Yours Reverently

*For my father, mother and family, and
for all who heard and read, or will read
the words of the Vicar*

Yours Reverently

...from the pulpit, the pub
and the *Parish Notes*, 1948-1953

Rev. O.L. Willmott (1910-1996)

Edited by Michael Willmott
Illustrations by Andy James

Robin-John
Willmott

BSP

Michael
Willmott

First published by Bishop Street Press 1997
Reprinted March 1998
Reprinted September 1998
Reprinted December 1998

ISBN 0 9531802 0 4

Produced by Action Publishing Technology Limited, Gloucester
Printed in Great Britain

Contents

Rev. O. L. Willmott
(1910–1996)

Oliver Leonard Willmott was born in Frome, Somerset, and educated there. He took a great interest in the parish church, St. John's, becoming a server and also taking up his lifetime interest in bellringing. At first a career in journalism seemed ahead of him as he started working for the *Somerset Standard*, but he changed course and spent seven years in the Anglican monastery of Kelham. Again he changed course, tempering the strict high church training of Kelham, cut off from the world, with two further years' training at the Bristol Church Missionary Society. There his ministry was on the streets of Bristol, and in contact with missionary work across the world. After ordination as an Anglican priest at Exeter Cathedral he became curate of Totnes, briefly. But war broke out, and he became an Army Chaplain. At first he was posted to Northern Ireland. Soon after, he was put in charge of the chapel of the Duke of York's Military School at Dover, and then of the chapel of Dover Castle, where services continued despite heavy shelling as our forces invaded France. At that time he was Chaplain at Fort Darland, the Army's toughest prison.

All of this was before he 'retired to the country' to look after the souls of his flock of 1,100 villagers, from squire to humble widow. He was much more than a vicar: he was a countryman, and a person who helped create a special sense of community in the post-war years. He ran a small-holding with pigs, turkeys, geese, hens and a cow to support his wife and family of seven children. He chopped trees for his Tudor fireplace which had attracted him to the place first of all. He mowed the churchyard, assisted by his faithful wife. He held forth at early sessions in the local hostelries – the Marquis of Lorne and the Crown Inn, Uploders. He visited the sick, and collected tirelessly for the yearly Fête which earned huge sums for the maintenance of the church fabric – he saw this as a mission in itself. But he kept in contact with the outside world by talking to all newcomers, while scanning *The Times* and *The Daily Telegraph* voraciously to keep up with national and international events. He listened to, and later watched the News, five or six times a day.

The fruits of this wide and deep experience are to be found in the *Parish Notes*, which he wrote monthly for thirty-four years. They record local news of church, parish and locality in meticulous detail, but they are much more than a chronicle: they are a testimony to his Christian practice, to his deep theological convictions, to his Anglicanism based on a firm belief in practised ecumenicalism – 'Unity without union', he preached; to his love of all people (apart from a few opponents, with whom he was fair, but ruthless); to his love of flowers, beasts and birds; and above all to his deep rootedness in the quintessentially English life of 'the little hills of Dorset'. He was a remarkable man, who had an entertaining and idiosyncratic style, which makes the *Parish Notes* very amusing, enlightening and, at moments, deeply inspiring.

Preface

This book is culled from an unusual set of documents, written by one person from 1948–1982. 'Person' might have been a typing error for 'parson', but it isn't. The Vicar's belief in his job and life recognised no distinction between these rôles. He was both person and parson. The only contributions by other people to the *Parish Notes* of Loders, Dottery (and later Askerswell) were made by word of mouth to the Vicar. He absorbed the information, and put it into his own words. On a rare occasion he would permit someone else's paragraph to be included. The *Parish Notes* were never a parish magazine – they were his organ. This is a solo effort over thirty-four years, appearing once a month, with only one month missing – June 1949. (No-one has an explanation for this lapse.)

The *Parish Notes* were his medium. He tested his words out on his wife, then printed (and was sometimes damned). He had by the end written three quarters of a million words, chronicling the life of his three parishes of Loders, Dottery and Askerswell near Bridport in West Dorset. (Askerswell was added to Loders and Dottery in 1952.) The *Notes* were produced on two sides of foolscap, once a month. The format never changed. They were intended as a 'newsletter' for his flock of eleven hundred souls, but ended up as something greater: a personal testimony. At first 110 copies were sold, though mysteriously only 100 copies were at first typed. Then the *Parish Notes* spread, giving the Vicar a world-wide audience, which flattered him.

He started off his ministry to his three churches on a bicycle. Not much escaped his attention in his nine-miles-long ride. When not heading to his churches, he walked the lanes with his dog, in his word – 'sermonizing' – or just noticing things, or talking to all passers-by. He was never off duty, and was only seen without a dog-collar when engaged in sweaty activity, hewing wood or spreading manure. His *Parish Notes* extended well beyond the parochial. Indeed, if you can open your ears while reading, you will hear his voice offering sly commentaries on most human affairs. Underlying his human commentary is a deep-seated Christianity, allied with a wisdom which is sometimes found in pubs, just after opening time.

The chapter-headings used are intended to help the reader focus on matters that preoccupied the Vicar's mind. Some may be more interested in the social and political commentaries of the opening two chapters. Others might like to delve straight-away into The Church's Year, which is the core of the book. Others might be attracted by the challenging link between campanology, male chauvinism, and bibulousness. From bell-ringing to the rôle of Victorian fathers with interest in the pleasures of the vine and hops is a heady step to take. That chapter is a very quick, and funny read.

But the rest of the chapters have their purpose. They show there were many sides to his character. It is a book to be dipped into, and returned to. It is only selected from the first five years of the *Parish Notes* up until the Coronation of Queen Elizabeth II. Even here, items of interest have had to be ejected for the sake of the whole. There are twenty-nine more years to come. Loders was the centre of the parishes and the site of the Vicarage. Dottery and Askerswell have been proportionately represented as far as possible. Two photocopied volumes of the complete works can be viewed in Bridport Museum in the Local History Department.

The aim of this book is to celebrate the Reverend Oliver Willmott's delight in words, his perceptiveness about all manner of person, his sharp eye, and his highly personal point of view. Whether he was holding forth from the pulpit, or from the corner of The Crown or The Marquis of Lorne or Spyway or even The Blue Ball at opening time, he used words wittily and economically. Nothing needs be erased from what he wrote. Only the selection of the items has been made for the convenience of a modern reader approaching these village annals. 90% of the words are his own. The 10% which are editorial comment are distinguished by a different typeface. His headings weren't headings so much as the first few words of each item underlined. (Pages 202 to 204 show how the material went from the handwritten version, composed always at one sitting, to the typed version, cyclostyled in Bridport. Woe betide spelling mistakes or errors of punctuation by the lady typist.) Each chapter follows the chronological order of the original. The aim has been to leave the original intact, though one or two errors that might confuse the reader have been 'repaired'.

The illustrations by Andy James – a grandson by marriage of the Vicar – have been the outcome of a productive collaboration during a German holiday. We were celebrating a family wedding. Strangely, a Saxon church near Lubeck provided the inspiration for a robust artistic style, alongside an editorial interpretation of the Vicar's text. The ornaments and design of the West Door had strong associations with Loders. Fortunately, these views chimed in with the production ideas of The Choir Press, Gloucester, and in particular of Miles Bailey and Clive Dickinson. My thanks to family and friends who provided critical support and background information. My mother was an excellent 'secretary' since she knew all the secrets. Julian Pandya, a former colleague at Highfields School, Wolverhampton, provided essential historical information, and masterly inspiration. My sister Juliet and her husband David threaded through the text for inconsistencies, and provided invaluable advice about the tone and presentation of the whole work. This is not a biography, but inevitably there are some value judgements about the Vicar's life and character which are the editor's alone: only the Vicar can judge if there be any offence. First and foremost, this is a celebration of his memory.

Editorial notes

1. The words of the Vicar are in normal type. Any editorial comment is as typed on this page, or in square brackets [ ].

2. The Vicar's headings have been used where possible: where not, the Editor has endeavoured to make up an appropriate introduction.

3. On pages 207–211 there are some background facts about the period covered by the book, with cross-references to the text where possible.

4. The typing customs of 1950 were not the same as the typing customs of 1997. If there are any anomalies, we apologize.

CHAPTER I

In little

Dorset – England 1948–1953

Do the *Parish Notes* present a pastoral idyll, or a rural backwater, or the quiet murmur of country repose, or what? After the Second World War, West Dorset settled back into a peacefulness which had more resemblance to eighteenth century village life than to any twentieth century modernity. The village shop, with a weekly trip to Bridport, and perhaps an occasional excursion to Dorchester or Yeovil, satisfied people's consumer needs. The bicycle and bus had not yet been superseded by the private car. Farming and the Bridport net industry provided most people with employment. The Church, the village Hut, the School and the pubs produced the essential ingredients of rural culture. A trip to the Palace at Bridport to see a film, an outing to Weymouth, or a pilgrimage to Salisbury were quite momentous occasions. There was time to stand and stare. Matters of national importance often slipped by unnoticed. Otherwise, as in the comment on the Coronation by 'the aged widow of Loders' at the end of this chapter, the real world was kept at a wry distance.

So, here is a picture of post-Second World War rural England, with echoes of smuggling days and hints of things to come in the descriptions of radiogram recitals, central heating, and the Vicar's new car. The peacefulness alluded to above is never static. The Vicar revelled in odd happenings and had a great capacity to find new ways of reporting the commonplace. There is an attempt at logic in the selection of items to fit the eight chapters. The first chapter describes the small world of West Dorset just after the war whereas the second gives evidence of wider ripples. Some items defy logic and could fit a number of chapters.

A good start

Agricultural people have little time for reading. But we might have been saved our fears that these *Notes* would not be welcomed. Everybody seems to have read them, and people with indifferent sight say that the type is easy on the eyes. More than half of the parish have made an act of faith in paying for the *Notes* twelve months in advance. Our circulation manager is puzzled. 100 *Notes* only were printed, and 110 have been sold! Mrs. Harry Legg may know the answer. She, Miss Holmes, Mrs. Osborne and Mrs. Gale of Dottery, have shown unexpected talent as newsagents. Without them there would have been no *Notes*, and we are deeply grateful.

August 1948

St. Mary Magdalene and Lancelot Andrewes

The Dedication Festival is now a pleasant memory. Our lady decorators were on top of their form. Loders had not been used to a summer festival, and we did not know how graciously the old church could take to sweet peas, marigolds and gladioli. Congregations were good. They included a party from Dottery. A troop of Scouts from Coventry, who were in camp in the park, paraded at matins. Some of them were in church at five o'clock on the following morning, doing vigil before their institution as Rovers. The Rev. Lancelot Andrewes, of Oriel College, Oxford, who took part in the Dedication services, comes of an interesting family. One of his ancestors was the great Bishop Lancelot Andrewes of Winchester, who was the chief translator of the Authorised Version. Another was the famous 'Merry Andrew', physician to King James the First, who danced before the Court at the age of 108! Rev. Andrewes' brother, an admiral, is head of the naval department of the Imperial Defence College, and is an A.D.C. to King George VI.

August 1948

Records

About 12 baptisms, 8 weddings and 6 funerals take place in a year in Loders Church. It was therefore a record when the Vicar took four baptisms in one afternoon. On the last Saturday in August he took a wedding and two funerals within two hours, but the wedding and one of the funerals were at Bradpole. Even the Vicarage garden has made a record. It produced a potato (Majestic) weighing 2 lbs 10 oz – 9¼ ozs, heavier than the Catriona mentioned in the *Bridport News*. It made two meals for four people.

October 1948

An underground lake

There may be a good-sized lake beneath Waddon. The depth of the old well at the crossroads near Bell was lately increased from 33ft to 83ft. Some 36,000 gallons of water were pumped out in a short time, and the level in the well sank by less than half an inch. An engineer tested the vicinity of the well with a mechanical water-diviner, and came to the conclusion that a huge reservoir of water is there. The Parish Council may keep this in mind till the day when it is feasible to give the village an indoor water supply. Nothing takes the gloss off country life like fetching your water from a distance in all weathers, especially when there are several children to be tubbed.

November 1948

Loders Choir Social

One keeps hearing that Loders had a wonderful choir in the old days. The present choir is becoming a force in the parish. It gave us quite the happiest social it is possible to have, then it raised £9.2s. for the Church's Children's Society by two nights of carol singing, and so allowed the church-wardens to devote Christmas Day collections to church expenses instead of to the Society. The choir enjoyed their carol singing, 'spite of having to huddle together round Mr. Wells' tilley lamp to help the winter's rage to freeze their blood less coldly. "Sirs, the night is darker now", was true enough when somebody dropped the lamp. They were glad to be invited to sing in the warm bright hall of the Court, with Lady Le Breton listening in the background, and to end up with 'eats' round the old Tudor fireplace at the Vicarage. On the following night they lingered so long over refreshment provided at Matravers and Upton Manor that by the time they had worked back to Shatcombe the audience were mostly in bed. It is no small tribute to the charm of Miss Peggy Pitcher, the collector, that the choir garnered what they did.

January 1949

Loders Church

The Survey of the Royal Commission on Historical Monuments contains interesting details about Loders Church. It identifies the figures of the medieval glass in the south chapel as St. Barbara holding a tower, St. Dorothy with a basket and flowers, St. Leonard holding a manacle in his right hand, and a man of the fifteenth century with a staff and bag. It puts the date of the ancient door to the belfry at late 14th century. It does not agree with our guide book about the Easter Sepulchre in the chancel, and the medieval frescoes on the tower arch. It holds that the Easter Sepulchre is merely a recess tomb, and that the frescoes are 17th century. The survey says that Loders is remarkable for the number of its lynchets, i.e. hills artificially terraced for grazing.

January 1949

Radiogram recitals

Loders is not conspicuous for its appreciation of music, but it may be later on, if it turns out well to the radiogram recitals which the Women's Institute have arranged for the whole village on Tuesday, September 13th, Thursday, 22nd, and Thursday, 29th, at times to be announced later. The merits of the pieces played will be pointed out by Mr. Jeffries, a lecturer of Bristol University, who is also a 'cellist. The recitals will be in the Hut.

September 1948

A wish fulfilled

At the time of the Gymkhana, the Committee were wishing they could get hold of a film star to do the opening. Today, Loders has seven film stars to draw upon. They are, Mrs. J. Osborne, Mrs. H. Crabb, Mrs. Rogers, Mrs. Poole, Mrs. Greening, Mrs. H. Legg, and Mrs. F. Osborne, so there should be no difficulty about next year's opening ceremony. The seven achieved stardom in this wise. The chief cameraman of Wallace Productions Limited called at the Vicarage with a copy of *The Daily Mail*, which said that Loders was one of those villages where in sunny weather the wives could be seen sitting in the street making nets. He wanted to make a short film of this. Would the Vicar show him those streets where the wives would be making nets in the sunshine? The Vicar could not recollect such a sight, but assured the cameraman that his perambulations through the village were usually done in a reverie, and he might have seen it without knowing. Whereupon the cameraman whisked him through the village in a high powered car. But neither of them could see netmaking in the streets. The cameraman said *The Daily Mail* could not lie, so he arranged for the seven ladies, all expert net makers, to be at work on the pavement opposite the Loders Arms the following afternoon, when they were duly filmed. The cameraman said that the film would shortly be on view in many of the cinemas of Great Britain and Canada. Do not let this shake your faith in films. When a camera goes through a village, it sees what you cannot, and the camera cannot lie. Let us hope that the cameraman can't, either. He promised a donation to church funds.

October 1949

A declining population

Dr. Edersheim, Vicar of Loders, writing in his parish magazine in 1881 (he only wrote one magazine a year) observes that the census taken that year had shewn the population of the parish to be 952, which was a decrease from 1,115 in the census previous to that. The population of the ecclesiastical parish is now given as 632, and that of the civil parish cannot be much more than 450. Dr. Edersheim had the assistance of a curate, the Rev. W. P. Ingledow. Those were the palmy days of the Church.

November 1949

An old English Christmas

A gentleman who spent his Christmas with relations in Loders rightly said that one needs to be in a village to get the old spirit of Christmas. We did all that tradition demands. Our choir serenaded the village with carols shortly before Christmas, drinking sherry with their churchwarden en route, refuelling with some uncommonly powerful cocoa at a naval establishment out in the wilds of the parish, and ending up with a feast and ghost stories at the big fireplace of the vicarage. Matins on Christmas Day would have had the hearty approval of Sir Roger De Coverley. The Squire's party filled the chancel stalls, a very representative congregation filled the church, and when the children had sung carols round the Christmas tree, on the chancel step, they received packets of sweets from the tree, which they stoically refrained from eating till after service. On Boxing Day the Christmas scene was beautifully rounded off by the appearance of the Cattistock Hunt at Boarsbarrow. The best view was to be had from the summit of Boarsbarrow. There the spectators looked down, and saw the procession of redcoated huntsmen emerge from the lane, and fan out over the brown bracken of Loscombe. What they hoped to see, and did not, was

Reynard breaking cover. That sight was reserved for one pair of eyes alone. In the afternoon, when the Hunt and everybody else had gone, Sir Edward's nephew went shooting in Loscombe, and stepped on a fat old fox who was asleep in the very place the hounds had drawn. The bed was warm and deeply dented, indicating that it had been slept in for several hours. We suspend judgement until the mystery has been fully debated in the village inn.

January 1950

Mortality

A perusal of the burial registers shew that Mrs. Marsh was of a greater age than anybody buried in this parish since 1813. We cannot say how she compares with others previous to 1813 because the burial registers only began in 1813. Before that, there was no record kept of individual burials. The churchwardens accounts merely gave the number of burials in a year. Mrs. Marsh's nearest rivals were: Matthew Salisbury, 98, buried in 1906; Diana Hansford, 96, buried in 1832; and Amelia Brown, 96, buried in 1945. The burial registers are shocking evidence of the infant mortality rate in the 19th century. There are two successive pages of burials in which every entry except one is of a child under eight, and the exception is a girl of twenty. The infant mortality rate in Loders began a marked decline in the Great War, and now child burials are the exception instead of the rule. When we shudder at the awful forces of destruction science has let loose in the world, we must remember what it has done for mothers and infants.

January 1950

A fox from his lair

The Cattistock Hunt were rewarded for giving Loders a second chance after drawing a blank at Boarsbarrow on Boxing Day. When they met recently at Matravers Corner, they started a fox right away, and thereafter so many foxes that they did not know which to follow. It is a healthy sign of the times that many more farmers follow the hunt.

February 1950

Tantalising!

At midday on a recent Saturday, the Bridport Fire Brigade and a wedding reached Loders together in a great hurry. The wedding was for the church, and was ten minutes late. The fire brigade was for a house near the church, which had a chimney ablaze. Fate had managed things badly in giving simultaneously two such absorbing spectacles to a village in which nothing ever happens. It was a strain on local eyes and necks to give both events the attention they deserved, and it is feared that much of interest went unobserved.

February 1950

Rook pie

Ninety-five rooks fell to the guns of the recent shooting party at Loders Court. The shooting is an annual event whose drawing power, judging by the number of spectators, is on the increase. Next day the village dined on rook pie. A newcomer to this dish found it edible in a high degree – not quite up to partridge, but superior to pigeon. The village wives can turn six rooks into a pie ready for the oven in half an hour.

June 1950

St. Mary Magdalene, the village feast

Loders Feast used to be kept up for a whole week round about July 22nd, the festival of St. Mary Magdalene, patron saint of Loders. One of the objects of the feast was to thank God for the lovely old church of Loders. If we cannot revive the picturesque externals of the Feast – the fun fair and the dancing in the street – we can, and ought to, continue the annual thanksgiving for Loders Church. It is a thing of beauty which has come down to us through the centuries, the 'rude forefathers of the hamlet' sleep beneath its walls, and it is the ancient place where God and Loders meet. This year we shall keep the Feast on Sunday, July 23rd. We shall decorate the church, and trust that all Loders may come to give thanks for their mother church. Last year's observance was encouraging.

July 1950

Hail and farewell

P.C. William Edrich and family have taken the place of P.C. Trevett and family at Loders Police Station. If Constable Edrich can win the hold on village affection that Constable Trevett had, he will do well. Constable Trevett has moved to Wimborne, where he reckons to add another two years to his thirty already spent in the Force. He will be within easier reach of his home town of Sherborne, and his wife of hers, which is Bournemouth. Constable Trevett had been stationed four years in Loders. Our recollection will be of a neighbourly policeman who recovered errant goslings, and quelled midnight roysterers with a look, who, in the relaxation of his own fireside could tell tales of mystery and horror; for, as Gilbert & Sullivan testify, a policeman's lot is not a happy one. Constable Edrich is newer to the Force. He has been stationed at Dorchester for the last three years. He has a wife and two surviving children, and his grandfather is also living with him. We trust that the move to the country may improve the health of the new Constable and his family. He came straight to Loders from hospital, where he had had pneumonia. Mrs. Edrich left hospital a week before he went in.

August 1950

£10 for a sermon

Richard Travers, in his will proved 26th June, 1815, left 'To the Vicar of Loders £10. If not in residence, to the Curate at the time, for a sermon on the Sunday after my burial. It is desired that no comments or praise be given of the deceased, only let it be a common practical discourse to warn others to prepare to pay the same debt. My wish is to be buried on the north side of the our family tomb, next the chancel, where my dear good mother was buried.' Any vicar in these days of high prices and low clerical stipends would find it hard to comply with the direction of this will not to praise a man who was willing to pay £10 for a sermon.

September 1950

Fireworks on Boarsbarrow

Sir Edward Le Breton and Mr. R. Pitcher are allowing the children to let off their fireworks on Boarsbarrow on November 5th. When the children pool their fireworks in this way, they get a better show, as was proved by the communal celebration on Waddon last year.

November 1950

Hats off to the Young Farmers

It is a safe bet that our Young Farmers will win the Gardiner Loving Cup for their harvest supper in the Ex-Servicemen's Hut. Even Miss Sally Barnes, of the Beaminster Club, who was a guest, is not entirely unwilling to consider the possibility of this. The dinner was as delectable as ever, the decoration of the hut was better than it had ever been, and the entertainment which followed the dinner could not be bettered. It was unabashedly rustic, and the audience at once caught on to the fun that the performers were having with it. By the way, the shudder which passed through the high table when the Loyal toast was drunk had no political significance. It had something to do with the lack of sugar in the elderberry wine.

November 1950

Smuggling

The late Mrs. L. A. Bartlett, who died at the home of a daughter in Wimborne, and was buried in Loders churchyard after an impressive service in the church, was a member of a family

which had held the licence of the Crown Inn, Uploders contin-
uously, since it was built, some 200 years ago. At one time she
may well have been the youngest licensee in England, for both
her parents having died, the licence was transferred to her at
the age of 19. Her husband pre-deceased her by 23 years, so
she had the distinction of holding the licence in all three of
woman's estates – as spinster, wife, and widow. The family
have kept the licence unblemished for two centuries, but Mrs.
Bartlett could recall stories she had heard from her parents of
raids by the Excise men in search of smuggled liquor. By all
accounts, while the Excise men were wasting their energy on
the Crown, the neighbouring wives were in their cottages
'sitting pretty' on kegs of brandy, for which their voluminous
skirts were 'just the job'. To the end of her life Mrs. Bartlett
was a model of industry. She kept her whole family of eight
surviving children, and her in-laws, in knitted hose.

December 1950

A paradox

As times grow harder, and money gets tighter, the annual tea and
entertainment given by Sir Edward and Lady Le Breton to the
youth of the village, seems to become more sumptuous. As a gale
roared outside, the young folk of Loders sat in the noble dining
room of the Court, at tables loaded with sugared doughnuts,
cream buns, iced buns, and pyramids of pink and white
meringues. The children had come in from the billiard room,
where they had been highly entertained by a Bournemouth
conjuror. When the feasting was done, and cheers for the host
and hostess had been called by Frank Good, the children went
through the hall to the motor coach which was to take them
home, but Father Christmas waylaid them, and bestowed on each
guest an orange, chocolate biscuits, crackers, and a half-crown.

January 1951

Rustic Christmas

The Parish Party was an unqualified success. Nearly all the families in Loders were represented at it, and so many came from Dottery that they had to engage the town bus to carry them. The competition for the best disguise attracted many entries, and lent colour to the assembly. Had the criterion of judgement been the prettiest dress, or the most original the judges would have found a decision difficult to come by, but the winner was the one who was the last to be recognised by the audience. This turned out to be Mrs. Harper, of Uploders. She was wearing an old dress uniform of a major of the King's Own Highland Regiment, and with the help of fierce moustachios she cut a very military figure indeed. It is said that the uniform once belonged to Major Bradwell, of Loders Court. The high light of the evening was the appearance of the Symondsbury Mummers, whose play on the floor of the hut occupied a full hour. They gave us a pleasing sample of the fun made at Christmas by the rustics of the Middle Ages. We trust that the frothy tankards of ale brought in by three stalwart men of Loders, when the Master Mummer called for small beers, were to the Mummers' taste. Refreshments were abundant, and seemed to be circulating throughout the latter part of the evening. If some people missed their ham sandwich, it was the Vicar's fault. Forgetting that they were in limited supply, he fed them to the Mummers lavishly. But they deserved it.

March 1951

The Notes

Rising costs of production have made these humble Notes a bedfellow with the illustrious *Dorset Echo* and *Bridport News*. When our financial year ends in July, our price will have to be 2½d. The cost of our paper has been doubled, and our small profit has been turned into a loss. Even with that, we suspect that our printers are letting us down very lightly.

March 1951

Hard work never killed anybody

Men like the late Mr. William Marsh, of Pymore, are fast dying out, and their equals in capacity for work will never be seen again. Mr. Marsh, who was a native of Loders, began work at the age of nine, and kept it up till seventy-five, with scarcely a day off for illness. The work was heavy work, too, in Pymore Mills. Nobody would like to see a return to those conditions, and yet the puzzling fact is that these old men, with long hours and small pay, are invariably happier than younger men with short hours and big pay, and seem to get more out of life. If proof were needed that hard work never killed anybody, Mr. Marsh was it. He died at 86. His brother-in-law, Mr. Albert Hyde, who also worked from a child at Pymore Mill, and walked to his work from Loders at six in the morning, has just thrown off a serious illness, and is downstairs again. His age is not far short of Mr. Marsh's.

July 1951

Good news!

A Lyme Regis firm has undertaken to instal tubular heating beneath the seats in Loders Church. Many necessary formalities have to be observed before anything can be done in a church, but it looks as if we may be warm this winter.

July 1951

Teachers in short supply

A second teacher has been obtained for Loders School, thanks to the good offices of a 'friend at court'. It was not an easy acquisition. Teachers are in very short supply. The effect of raising the school leaving age to fifteen before there were enough teachers to cope with the increased school population has been to lower the standard of education all round.

July 1951

Vikings marooned

The Sunday School children went to Lyme Regis and Sidmouth for their outing, in two coaches. The day was full of thrills. At

Lyme Regis they tried the roundabouts, dodgems, and swing boats, while some took to sea in a motor boat, and rode the waves like young Vikings. They left Lyme in the afternoon, and the biggest thrill was to come – the back axle of one of the coaches broke on a steep hill near Honiton. This coach carried most of the children, and they were more than delighted; for word had gone round that they would be marooned too long to start school in September. But their hope was short lived. The first coach, which had emptied its load in Sidmouth and returned, and a relief bus from Chard, arrived together. The marooned ones joined the others at tea in Sidmouth. Mrs. Willmott and the Sunday School wish to thank the parish for giving so generously to the outing, and to Miss Hinks and Mrs. G. Gale for collecting. The collection amounted to nearly £17.

September 1951

The skill of the South-Western Electricity Board

The electrical heating apparatus for Loders Church will prove more expensive than the original estimate. The electrician who has the work in hand reported to the Church Council that a four-core cable would be necessary to carry the extra current required into the church. It was a shock to the Council to learn that this length of cable, and the laying of it, would add about £110 to the bill. Fortunately, the proceeds of the recent fete were available, and these were voted into the heating fund. The South-Western Electricity Board have laid the cable, and the electrician can go ahead with the business of wiring, and fitting a tubular heater to each pew. But only the Secretary of the Church Council knows what formalities have to be dealt with, and what girding and goading has to be done, before work like this can begin. We have hope that the electric heat may be in well before Christmas. A word of appreciation of the men of the South-Western Electricity Board is not amiss here. They had great care for the appearance of the church path when they dug their long trench for the cable, and they dealt reverently with all the human remains they brought to light. They removed and replaced Mr. David Crabb's fine border of ageratum so skilfully that not one plant died, and, if anything, they left the path neater than they found it.

October 1951

Lucky children

We say, with excusable conceit, that no parish is kinder to its children than Loders. The teachers and parents of the day school gave their children a breaking-up party which they will not soon forget. Jelly seems to figure large in the child's idea of paradise, and here there were great bowls of it, of colours and consistencies to suit all palates. There was also a Christmas tree, and a Santa Claus to give out its presents. On Christmas morning the children requited the grown-ups by singing four carols from the chancel. Here there was another tree, which the Mothers' Union had hung with sweets, and each child received a packet before leaving the chancel. The children's partying reached its grand finale at what is commonly called 'The Court party'. This party is aptly named, first because it is held at Loders Court, and second, because the hospitality that the Squire and his Lady have meted out for the past thirty years is right royal. The party was true to form in beginning with a conjuring display. But this time it began a bit late; for the magician was held up by a rally of motor cyclists outside Loders Hut, and only a threat to turn the offenders into caterpillars got him through. After the magic came a sumptuous tea in the dining room. Some seventy children and parents sat down to it, noting with satisfaction that one of the hunting trophies on the wall, a tiger, had not forgotten to put on his top hat in honour of the occasion. One intelligent child asked why the magician needed to join in eating the children's buns when he was so clever at producing his own out of his hat. When crackers had been pulled, Frank Good voiced the thanks of the company to Sir Edward and Lady Le Breton, making feeling reference to the heavy cost of parties like this. The children left the Court and boarded the bus that was to take them home, each the richer by a half-crown.

January 1952

Askerswell joins Loders and Dottery

Canon Daniell, who became Rector of Askerswell in 1941, resigned the benefice on the 31st January last, because of ill health. He remains Rector of Litton Cheney and Rector of Chilcomb. The Diocesan Pastoral Reorganisation Commission decided some months ago that at the next vacancy the Rectory of Askerswell should be offered to the Vicar of Loders, and that thenceforward the churches of Askerswell, Loders and Dottery should be served by the Vicar of Loders. This decision has not yet been ratified by the Church Commissioners, but their approval is as certain as anything in this world can be. Meanwhile, the Bishop has made the Vicar of Loders responsible for Askerswell, pending his institution and induction as Rector. Two points need noting. First, the new arrangement does not mean that Askerswell and Loders become one parish. Askerswell remains a self contained and independent parish until such time as it may have a resident Rector again, and the proceeds of the sale of the Rectory have been put by to build him a new house. The second point is that the Reorganisation Commission did not wish the incumbent of Loders to bear the burden of three churches. Its own proposal was that when Loders took over Askerswell, Dottery should go to Allington, giving the incumbents concerned two churches each. But Loders and Dottery refused to be parted, Askerswell clamoured to join the pigeon pair, and the Commission gave them their way. So we have only ourselves to blame if some of the services in the three churches are at inconvenient times. The inconvenience may be slight, and there is no reason why we should not be a happy family. From now onwards the time of services will be experimental, until we can see what is best.

February 1952

Harvest supper at Eggardon

Harvest Festival is about to begin, as these *Notes* go to press. The offer of Loders Choir to do an anthem at Dottery has been gladly accepted. The Choir have prepared another anthem for Loders Harvest on October 12th. Kindly note that the Harvest

Evensong at Loders will be at 6 p.m. Askerswell Choir also have an anthem for their Harvest on October 5th. The Askerswell Harvest Evensong will be at 7 p.m. Wing. Com. and Mrs. Newall revived a nice old country custom by inviting their farm workers and helpers to a harvest supper. A company numbering two dozen sat down to a feast by candlelight in the ancient dining hall of South Eggardon, and then moved from the past to the present by adjourning to the drawing room to see and laugh over home-made films of their own harvesting. Farmer Barnes of Dottery, used to be keen on maintaining the custom of harvest supper, holding it in his farmyard at Bilshay when the last load of corn came in. Now he is content, year by year, at a Christmas party which is a pale ghost of its former self, to sing the old song, 'If I could plant one tiny seed of love in the garden of your heart,' with both eyes on our own Mrs. Gale.

October 1952

A notable induction

For those who can concentrate on the business in hand, and be aware at the same time of irrelevant details, the recent induction of a new Rector of Askerswell by the Bishop of Sherborne was of unusual interest. First, the large congregation contained a gentleman who is 106 years old. Nobody would have guessed that, for he looks only half his age. He is an uncle by marriage of Dr. Waight, Curate of Bridport. The only outward evidence of his great age is deafness. The other item of interest was the evidence the service gave of what the collection means to a good churchwarden. Our churchwardens simply lost control of themselves in the presence of so much potential revenue. They made two distinct attempts to get in the collection before the sermon. None of the violent signals from the chancel could restrain them, and when they sat down to listen to the Bishop it could be seen in their faces, that satisfaction at having reaped half the collection was fighting with anxiety for the half unreaped. Their zeal made a profound impression on the Lord Bishop.

October 1952

A good harvest

Our three churches can look back on their harvest festival
services with the satisfaction that the farmer feels – but, of
course, would not express – about this year's harvest.
Decorations were exceptionally beautiful, congregation's were
very large, and hymns and anthems were sung as if they were
really meant. At Dottery the corn crosses beside the altar were
evidence that Mrs. Wensley had recovered from her lengthy
illness; at Askerswell the focal point was a small sheaf of corn,
standing impressively alone at the chancel step, with a bunch
of grapes at its waist (one wondered whether a bottle of olive
oil might be hidden beneath its skirts to complete the
psalmist's catalogue of human needs, corn, wine and oil). At
Loders the special appeal for flowers brought dahlias and prize
chrysanthemums in magnificent response. There was also an
abundance of eggs, both at Dottery and Loders. These were
distributed to old and sick people of the parish, whose pleasure at receiving them, though great, did not equal that of
those who took them round. It was for the latter a blessful
experience to be distributing for the church instead of collecting. Loders again achieved the distinction of filling the church
both morning and evening. At both services the Vicar, while
preaching, managed to precipitate a pulpit apple into the lap of
a lady sitting beneath. The gentleman who is reported to have
said, quoting Scripture, at the Travellers' Rest, 'Fancy he
tryin' to tempt thy wife wi' a h'apple', will find, if he looks
up Genesis, that the alleged apple was Eve's weapon.

November 1952

A year of achievement

In wishing our readers a happy new year, we may be forgiven
a reference to the year just ended. From many angles 1952 was
a year to be thankful about. Askerswell roused itself, and
raised a gross sum of about £1 per head of the population
(1931 census) to get its church out of debt, and to furnish the
churchwarden with a working balance. Loders got well ahead
in what is proving to be a minor restoration of the church. The
old lead patched beyond endurance was replaced by one of

Welsh slate and bitumen, decayed timbers were renewed, and sound ones treated with preservative. The plaster ceiling was made safe for many years (we hope) and the interior of the church redecorated. A handsome screen of leaded lights was put in the tower arch, and that now makes it possible for the temperature of the church to be raised to fifty degrees, within a few hours, when it is freezing outside. This minor restoration was paid for out of the accumulated proceeds of church fêtes, and by a lucky sale of scrap lead at a time when it was fetching a phenomenal price. The kitty is now empty, but as the work is not finished, Loders still faces a substantial bit of money raising before its priceless old church is fully restored. Nearly all the windows need re-leading, much of the stonework needs repointing, and then there is the organ. As played by Mr. Tiltman, you would think the organ was in perfect condition. But ask the tuner. Each time that gentleman gets to work on it, he reports that it is greviously ill. All the pipes are half choked with dust, several do not function at all, the bellows have come unstuck, and how the venerable machine manages to hold together is a mystery. The makers of byegone days knew their job, or their handiwork would not have lasted so long and be still worth mending.

January 1953

Court party

Loders children know from long experience that when the Christmas parties are over and gone all is not lost, for the biggest party, that given by Sir Edward and Lady Le Breton at Loders Court, is still to come. This party, in early January, was on traditional lines. About sixty children met first in the billiard room for a display of magic by a Bristol conjuror, and then moved to the still greater delights of a tea in the dining room. Freedom from parental oversight, and the connivance of host and hostess, enabled them to get to grip right away with the meringues, iced buns and doughnuts without the preliminary skirmish with bread and butter, and such was the abundance of the former that no room remained for the latter; bread and butter was like gold in the reign of Solomon – nothing thought of. A young voice stilled the din of cracker-pulling to thank Sir Edward and his lady for their hospitality. It spoke feelingly of the cost, and included in the thanks the use the youth of the village were allowed to make of the billiard room in winter and the tennis court in summer. Clutching apples, oranges and halfcrowns, the children made for the gate, where a coach was waiting to take the distant ones home.

February 1953

Fire-fighting in Uploders

A chimney caught fire in Uploders, and was put out eventually by Bridport Fire Brigade. The account of it given by the house-holder concerned, runs something like this:- 'Yes, there it were, a blaxin' away. I fought un till a get out o' me reach, then I went to the front door, and waited for the carrier to pass by. He were late that marning, but I axed un if a wouldn't mind when a were in Bridport ta call at the Vire Station, and axe 'em to come out. He said a would, but a had a vew parcels to deliver first. When the Viremen come, they said they thought 'twas a 'oax'. They told I to be sure and zend 'em a registered letter next time.'

March 1953

Ancient and modern

An aged widow of Loders, too infirm to go out, and living alone under the thatched roof of a dilapidated cottage, shewed the difference between ancient manners and modern in her atti-tude to the Coronation. Having decorated the small window of her only downstairs room, on June 2nd, she arrayed herself in her Sunday best, drew up her chair to her wireless set, and sat before it with clasped hands, as in church. She did not reckon to be seen by anybody. When our roving reporter called on her, she said, in a whisper, 'This is all very solemn, isn't it?'

June 1953

CHAPTER 2

At large

Dorset – England 1948–1953

Half a century earlier, Thomas Hardy noticed that the train taking milk to London from Dorchester, and bringing back news from the capital, was the only real invader from the outside world. In 1948, only the telephone and the 'wireless' (as the Vicar insisted on calling it) made inroads into the rural consciousness. Even when television arrived, and cars speeded up the pace, for a good quarter of a century rural life remained slow, obeying the rhythms of the seasons and responding to the Church's year rather than to the pressure of national, let alone world events. When Queen Elizabeth II was crowned, the most remembered sign of the times may well have been the free gift of a commemoration mug to all those at the village Fête. At her coronation there were three televisions in Uploders, and one in Loders. Only as farm labouring became more mechanized and fewer workers were needed did estate cottages become retirement homes, and village life changed its shape.

The sequence of the Vicar's news meanders amongst the inconsequential (see his hurt pride as he receives no preferential treatment while waiting in The Sausage Queue) and the gravely serious. It usually ends up with something comical.

HMS *Vanguard*

Some Bridport people had difficulty in getting aboard *H.M.S. Vanguard* while she was in Weymouth bay. Loders people were lucky in having a friend at court in the person of Commander Streatfield, who is gunnery officer of the Vanguard. He showed a charabanc party from Loders and Symondsbury over his ship, including the royal apartments. It seems that he gave his guests a sumptuous tea in the wardroom, and pressed all the available ship's officers into service as waiters. The guests enjoyed the tea most in retrospect: the chocolate éclairs followed too closely on a choppy crossing from pier to ship. As gunnery Officer, Commander Streatfield will organise the ritual of 'crossing the line', on the Royal progress to Australia. It is whispered that he has secured the help of that wit Sir Alan Herbert and also of a Punch cartoonist.

October 1948

Burdens of office

Our Bishop, Dr. Lunt, has been ordered a complete rest. His formidable engagement list in the monthly diocesan gazette gave rise to fears that this might happen. Only the strongest can bear the present burdens of a bishop, and our Bishop may not be as strong as he looks. While he was with the troops in North Africa he contracted pneumonia and diptheria, both at once! That must have left its mark. As we remember George VI in his illness, we shall not forget our faithful Father-in-God.

December 1948

Life is like that

This month's *Sarum Messenger* was written by Dr. Lunt a few days before his sudden death. So we begin 1949 with a message from our Bishop, but without him. 'He, being dead, yet speaketh.' An hour before hearing the Bishop's death announced on the wireless, the Rector of Bridport received a letter from him, saying that he felt very fit, and that he was intending to come to Bridport the following week. Life is like that. We never know what a day may bring forth. If we are worldlings, this fact is melancholy. If we are trying to be worthy to be called into the presence of our holy and loving Father at any time, the fact is the opposite of melancholy.

January 1949

Imperial hand-outs

The food parcel that our fellow subjects of the King send us from overseas have convinced us, if we needed convincing, that the Empire is a good thing. We might temper our gratitude with a little pity for local voluntary workers who distribute the food. If, in the case of Loders, they should receive 120 tins of steak, i.e. one for each house, their job would be simple. But it often happens that there are, say, 40 tins of steak, 60 tins of carrots, and 60 tins of marmalade. At Christmas some most desirable food parcels arrived from South Africa – but only eight of them. Much of the food is perishable, and cannot be saved up for a future occasion. So the workers have to think out a fair distribution. When the recipients compare their gifts, the distribution may seem to be unfair, but if the recipients were in possession of all the facts, they would see that it was not. The workers do not take first choice. They accept with good grace what nobody else wants.

March 1949

The changing times

Once upon a time, the clerical collar ensured its wearer a compartment to himself in a railway carriage. Passengers would open the door, and step back hastily, as if they had seen a corpse in the compartment. Once upon a time, when a vicar walked through his parish, everybody fled indoors, and paralysis seemed to move along the street with his every step. Now it is different. The passenger steps into the compartment, sees the clerical collar, and exclaims, 'Ah, my luck is in – just the man!' And now the people who hang over the garden gate are not waiting for the daily paper or the postman. As likely as not, you hear them ask, 'Have you seen the Vicar up this way lately? I have been looking for him those last three days.' What is the cause of this wondrous transformation, that the clerical collar should be sought after? A revival of religion? Alas, no. The answer is 'Forms'. It is they that have made the clerical collar popular, because its wearer is privileged to testify that the form filler is what he makes himself out to be. Forms are much sworn at, but it may prove their passport to heaven that they gave many a dejected parson an agreeable sense that his people needed his services, and that he was able to do a thing for which they were grateful. But, you form-fillers, be not zealous overmuch! The cleric who was called out of the Bridport sausage queue to sign a form, never retrieved his place in the queue.

March 1949

Lest we forget

Remembrance Sunday is November 6th. A distinguished soldier of the Great War, Major-General Sir Harry Smith, is coming to Loders on that day to assist in the unveiling of the 1939–45 war memorial, and to give us an address. The service will begin at 10.45 a.m. – please note the time – so as to include the Silence, and the collection will be for Earl Haig's Fund. The new memorial should have been fixed and dedicated last year, but the Diocesan Faculty Court objected to certain details of the design, and alterations had to be made. The disappointment of last year will not be repeated this year; for the memorial has already been made, and will have been put in position immediately beneath the older memorial by the time these notes are in readers' hands. We owe it to the soldier who is coming from Wareham to crowd the church that morning, and, above all, we owe it to the glorious dead of both wars. 'At the going down of the sun, and in the morning, we will remember them.'

November 1949

Dr. William Anderson, D.S.O.

Our new Bishop, Dr. William Anderson, made his first official appearance in this Deanery when he instituted the new Vicar of Bothenhampton a few days ago. His fatherly manner, his fine voice, his suggestion of strength and stability, impressed us. He will be in continuous need of the two latter qualities if he is to stand up to the duties of a modern bishop, which have killed fine men ere now. Bishop Lunt had been a soldier bishop, winning the Military Cross in the Great War. Dr. Anderson is a sailor bishop, though he served as a combatant in the First King Edward's Horse in the Great War. In 1917 he was awarded the D.S.O. for action against enemy submarines.

November 1949

Boer War connections

We still hear appreciative references to the memorial service on Remembrance Sunday. Both Loders and Dottery turned out in strength, and were rewarded by a thoughtful address from General Sir Harry Smith. Nowadays it is hard to get buglers to sound Last Post and Reveille at these services, but having once heard our organist's substitute, the Dead March from Saul, we have lost our desire for buglers. The organ let us know that it was once the supplementary organ of Exeter Cathedral. We had at the service a veteran of the first Boer War in the person of Capt. Welstead. We fancy there is only one other Boer War veteran in the parish, and he is Mr. Frank Clark, of Uploders, who forgets his bad health and lights up with boyish glee when he recounts his adventures.

The four men of Dottery who died in the two wars are not named on the memorial plaque of their parish church of Loders as, strictly, they should be. But the Dottery church-wardens have ordered a memorial tablet for Dottery Church, and it will be ready shortly.

December 1949

An object for the next Fête? – Loders halt

Sir Eustace Missenden, chairman of the Railway Executive, announced, on November 22nd, British Railways' intention of closing down many small stations, in the interests of economy. We suspect that this may be the reason why British Railways are stone-walling local efforts to get a Loders Halt. Would it strengthen the hand of the Parish Council if they could offer to defray the cost of making a halt? The site was given long ago. Feeling in the village is such that people would rather raise the money for the Halt themselves than be baulked of it. How about a summer fête in aid of Loders Halt? The saving in taxi fares would make it a sound proposition.

December 1949

Looking ahead

The *Bridport News* reported that a site had been chosen, off New Road, for a new school to serve Askerswell and Loders. What it did not report was that the Dorset Education Committee does not expect this school to be built before circa 1965. Meanwhile, our school managers are going ahead with improvements to the existing school. The roof has been repaired, and the big classroom re-decorated, the outside is about to be repainted, and plans have been passed for an internal water supply with wash-basins. The new school may never materialise. It is hard to see the wisdom of building a new expensive school when a small outlay on the old schools would modernise them; and of deliberately increasing the number of scholars who would live at a distance from school. Today there is too much enthusiasm for new schools, and too little for new houses. The parish would rise up in righteous wrath if the authorities tried to give us a new school before they give us new houses.

February 1950

Workers' Playtime

Two young ladies who were at the Shrove Tuesday social told their mother it was the best ever. Colds, and general election activities, slightly reduced the number present, but the extra room for manoeuvre was welcome. This social was the choir's effort to raise funds for their summer outing, and it made a profit of about £10. It had more than the usual quota of set entertainment. Mr. Roy Poole led the singing of songs which were new to the sedate people, but which the multitude (who seem to listen to something called 'Worker's Playtime') took up with gusto and enjoyed immensely. The choir sang some songs, including a very local adaptation of the Vicar of Bray, and Mr. Harold Brown gave two delightful violin solos. Roars of laughter were raised by a shadowgraph play, depicting a bicycle accident, a surgical operation, and the sequel. This was put on by the Misses A. and J. Scott, V. Legg, and Mrs. E. Bishop. The Choir challenged a team consisting of Ringers and Women's Institute to a pancake race. Ringers and W.I. were under a considerable handicap. Their stove was nothing like as hot as the Choir's, and playful spectators kept stealing their fat and batter. Luckily for the Ringers, Mr. Harold Brown tossed his pancake to the floor, and his fat into the Choir stove, which then acquired a habit of bursting into flame, and gave Ringers and W.I. an easy win. Music for dancing was supplied, to everyone's satisfaction, by Mr. Billy Darby, and our organist, Mr. Bill Tiltman, made a successful debut as M.C. A Competition for grocery (given by Mrs. Brown) was won by Mrs. Chard, and for a cake (given by Mrs. Willmott) by Mrs. Rice-Oxley. Mr. Oscar Gale was at his usual post of door steward. Mrs. Harry Legg, who was in charge of the refreshments, conjured up a prodigious array of cakes and jellies, and added – we know not how – £2. 6s. 0d. to the profits. Her helpers were Mesdames R. Drake, B. Osborne, S. Hyde, F. Taylor, W. Gill, F. Crabb, C. Chard, P. Darby, H. Bishop, and R. Pitcher. Requests have been made for a mid-Lent social. We will see whether it can be arranged.

March 1950

Dottery's electoral position

The General Election [February, 1950] drew attention to the curious position of Dottery. Although the Allington Polling Station was easily the nearest – and Dottery is in the civil parish of Allington – the people of Dottery had to vote at Symondsbury. Why should these things be? And who substituted the inelegant name of 'Dottery' for its proper name, 'West End of Loders'?

April 1950

B.B.C. godfather

Mr. Ralph Wightman, the well-known Broadcaster, was recently in Loders Church. He stood godfather to Stuart Ascott.

May 1950

B.R. final decision

Loders Halt is now a full stop. The offer of the Parish Council to build the Halt themselves has been declined by the Railway Executive, whose letter, dated March 3rd, was passed round the Annual Parish Meeting for all to read. It said, 'The potential revenue to be derived from the Halt would not be sufficient to justify the capital expenditure which would be involved and to meet the annual charges which would arise; it is regretted that the way cannot now be seen to proceed further with the scheme.' A letter from the M.P. was also passed round the Meeting. It appears that when the Railways belonged to private companies, questions about them could be asked in Parliament. Now that they belong to the Nation, questions about them in Parliament are not allowed. The Halt, therefore, is not likely to materialise, and the Council is trying to improve the bus service.

May 1950

Overheard in Dottery

Lady, looking up from newspaper: 'Bless my soul! The other day York Minster was asking for a quarter of a million, now they want a hundred thousand for Salisbury spire. They never stop begging. We want that money on our children's backs and feet.' In another column of the same newspaper it was stated that in 1948–9 Britain spent £1,510 millions on tobacco, drink, cinemas, theatres and betting. The lady saw nothing remarkable in this. Those who think God is getting more than His share should ponder the recent discovery of a statistician, that the nation spends more in a year on matches than it does on religion.

July 1950

An unexpected meeting

The congregation were filing out of church one Sunday morning. A stranger among them made for the Vicar. 'Can you tell me the name of that man who read the lesson?' 'Sir Edward Le Breton,' said the Vicar. 'What a small place the world is,' said the stranger! 'When I came back from India on the troopship Nestor, after the 1914 war, he was in command of the men on board. I never expected to meet him here.'

July 1950

Increased profit

The object of the Fête is as much social as financial, but it is useless to pretend we are not pleased that last year's handsome profit was maintained and even exceeded by £1.7s.8d., this year's figure being £143.14s.5d. The optimists among us thought that £100 profit was as much as we could expect, because money gets tighter each year, and the end of clothes and points rationing has knocked the bottom out of the market for jumble provisions. Yet, with the exception of the jumble stall, which made only half of what it did last year, all the stalls were up, the sideshows were up, and so were the gymkhana, and the dance. The tea takings, at £32.6s.6d. were a record.

September 1950

Collective thanks

While the collecting for the Fête was at its height, Miss Hinks, Mrs. Bunnel, Miss Janet Symes and Mrs. Gale (Dottery) were brave enough to go collecting for the Sunday School outing. It says much for their persuasiveness, and for the warm hearts of the parishioners, that they got £17.7s.6d. They were followed a little later by members of the Women's Institute, selling flags for the Lord Mayor's Thanksgiving Fund. This fund is to thank the countries of the Empire for sending us £80 million of food parcels. There is something to be said for the theory of Miss Holmes (late president of the W.I.) that one could collect £10 a week in Loders for any worthy cause.

September 1950

Disappointed

The party which Dottery children were to have had at the
Vicarage, and the gathering of Dottery congregation round the
Vicarage fire after the Loders carol service, both had to be
cancelled on account of scarlet fever, which put the Vicarage
in quarantine. Bridport had a minor epidemic of scarlet fever
before Christmas, affecting nearly all the Bridport schools. It
reached Loders on Christmas Day, when Janet Bond and Ruth
Willmott went down with it. These were taken to the Bridport
Isolation Hospital. Then it caught Mr. Bond, Godfrey Elliott
and Evelyn Elliott, who could not go to hospital because it was
full. At the time of going to press, Loders is in a state of mild
alarm. Parishioners who suffer from a morbid fear of germs
have boxed themselves up, and those who would like to be in
the fashion are borrowing the Vicarage thermometer.

January 1951

A pillar of the church without pillars

Mrs. Eliza Jane Marsh of Pymore Terrace, who was buried at
Dottery, used to be a member of Dottery choir, and a decora-
tor of festivals. She was also one of those who collected money
for the building of Dottery Church. Her most treasured possession was a letter from King George VI congratulating her and
her husband William (now in his 87th year), on the diamond
wedding they celebrated 18th Feb. 1950. The letter is framed,
and hangs over the fireplace.

January 1951

Now the Vicar has four wheels

The Vicar writes: 'I have had the good fortune to inherit a car.
May I, through these *Notes*, thank all the kind people who
have given me, and my family, lifts, and sometimes lent me
their car? I am loth to mention names when I am indebted to
so many, but I really must acknowledge my gratitude to Mr. &
Mrs. Cecil Marsh, who, for nearly four years,have fetched me
to Dottery Church on wet Sundays, involving them each time
in a double journey of twelve miles.'

February 1951

Houses before schools

The Archbishop of York [Cyril Garbett] will be strongly supported in his request that houses should be built before new schools. We see timber, bricks, cement and other materials in short supply being lavished on the building of a new grammar school in Bradpole. Yet in our country schools, notably Loders and Askerswell, we have perfectly good classrooms that are empty. Why cannot the empty classrooms be put into use again, and the building of new schools be suspended until the housing problem is solved? Some quarters are making it a matter of congratulation that new palaces of learning are being built in hard times like these, but future generations will question our sanity when they find that we built palaces of learning, and left the teachers who taught in them homeless, and the children who learnt in them with overcrowded homes. We are under a moral obligation to find our own school teachers a house, but we haven't yet succeeded.

February 1951

Easter statistics and trade unions

The Prayer Book asks all confirmed members of the Church to make their Communion on Easter Day. In practice, about two and a half million do so. The compilers of statistics perversely insist on limiting the membership of the C. of E. to these. They ignore the fact given by the latest Registrar returns that 67 out of every 100 children in England are baptised in the Church of England, and that 70 out of every 100 couples married in England are married in the Church of England. These figures suggest that the nominal memberships of the C. of E. is about 70% of the population. Trade Unionists and members of the C. of E. have this in common, that they do not bother to attend their meetings.

March 1951

The *Notes* and inflation

Annual subscriptions to these *Notes* are due for renewal next month. We regret that the rising tide of prices has raised them from 2/-, to 2/6d. The sea is as salt for sprats as it is for

whales, and we find our circumstances the same as the big
daily papers, who have raised their prices. they have given up
trying to play Canute, and we are not starting.

June 1951

Loders School

The workmen are now putting in a hot and cold water supply,
which is pumped from the well in the playground by electric
motor, and chlorinated. As the number of pupils has gone up
to 28, we are entitled to a second teacher, and although teachers are in short supply, strong efforts will be made to get one.

June 1951

Primate down under

We do not realise how huge a success was the Archbishop of
Canterbury's [Geoffrey Fisher] recent tour of Australia and
New Zealand. Mr. Menzies, the Australian Prime Minister,
said that in his 22 years of public service he had never known
anyone have such enormous effect on the Australian people.
The Archbishop's speech to the Cabinet, he said, made a
profound impression. At one open air service in New Zealand
the congregation exceeded 30,000, and this, not in a farming
country like Haly, but a thinly populated agricultural country.
It was the first visit of an Archbishop of Canterbury to these
dominions.

June 1951

Council house philosophy

We discern two schools of thought about the council houses
which are to be built in Loders. One school demands as many
houses as possible, on the grounds that you cannot have too
much of a good thing, and that the cost of road and drainage
for eighteen houses is little more than the cost for six. The
other school urges restraint, on the ground that only eight
Loders people have applied for houses, and the outsiders who
would get the remainder of the houses would help make Loders
a dormitory of Bridport, and increase the danger of Loders

being drawn into the Borough and suffering a steep rise in rates as a consequence.

August 1951

Foreign visitors

The personnel of Loders is always changing. Old faces go, and new ones come in their place. Mr. George Ellery's cottage, smartened almost beyond recognition, is now occupied by Mrs. Edwards, a widow, lately come from Swanage. The Upton farm cottage which Mr. Lenthall has reconditioned and made so attractive, houses a new tractor driver and his family. It is probably the first time that that cottage has been the home of somebody who is not English. Its walls now listen to unfamiliar names, for the tractor driver is a Latvian, Bruno Enerts, his wife is a German from Wilhelmshaven, and the baby rejoices in the name of Aia. Newcomers to the parish of a different sort are a baby daughter, born recently to Mr. & Mrs. Foote, of the Travellers' Rest, and a baby daughter, born some weeks ago to Mr. & Mrs. Burrell, of Gribb. Both babies are very bonny. Mr. & Mrs. A.N. Burrell reckon to be leaving Waddon Farm shortly.

September 1951

Detective Heslin, C.I.D.

Local devotees of crime literature take pleasure in the annual visit to the parish of Detective Heslin, of the C.I.D., who figured prominently in the Haigh murder. He and his family have spent a fortnight's holiday at the Loders Arms each year for many years, and this year's visit has just ended. The detective occasionally patronises the bar and proves himself an agreeable conversationalist, although on the subject of crime he refuses to be drawn. Loders agrees with him. He looks to his holiday here to add about eight pounds to his weight. Professional worries and a life of hectic activity rob him of this in due course, which is as well for the Loders Arms' stairs.

September 1951

Houses

Everybody agrees that there is need for some new houses in
Loders. A few families are overcrowded, and a few young
couples want homes of their own. But not everybody under-
stands the difficulties the Parish Council have to contend with
in getting these houses. It seems that the Rural Council
contemplates building eighteen houses in Loders. On the
surface this looks grand, but it might mean that the parish
would get none at all. Eighteen houses require a sizeable piece
of land, and the land the Rural Council has in mind is part of
a small holding whose compulsory purchase might be resisted,
perhaps successfully, by the owner. Legal processes are
lengthy, and while these were going on, the houses would
remain unbuilt. So the Parish Council decided to ask for a first
instalment of eight houses, the land for which has a prospect
of being obtained. The vexatious thing is that when these
houses come into being, the Parish Council will have no say
in the letting of them. Having been financed and built by the
Rural Council, they will be let by the Rural Council to those
in the Rural District whose need for houses is greatest. The
experience of Burton and Chideock suggests that Loders
people will be lucky if they get half the houses built here.

September 1951

Festival of Britain

Summer outings have made their final spurt. The Women's
Institute took member's children to West Bay for an afternoon,
Mrs. P. Symes took a coach load of sightseers to the Festival
of Britain in London, and the Mother's Union went to the
Weymouth Ritz to see the antics of Mr. Dixon. There is now
a difference of opinion among the Mothers as to whether Mr.
Dixon is entirely in good taste. But surely the fact that a
staunch churchwarden confesses to having seen Mr. Dixon's
act no less than four times settles the question?

September 1951

Musicians' Union

The winter activities of the parish organisations are getting into stride. All the efforts of the Young Farmers are directed towards their harvest supper; the Women's Institute faces its annual general election this month; and the Agricultural Discussion Club has gone into action with a membership of 70, and with the genial Mr. Wells as chairman. The Club wishes whist players to make a note of Wednesday, December 12th, when the grand Christmas whist drive will be held in the Hut. In mentioning the Hut, we are reminded that dances and entertainments are going to be much harder to arrange there than in the past. It seems that the Musicians' Union are in a position to insist, and are insisting, that dance music in the Hut shall in future be supplied by members of their union, or by gramophone records under licence. This will greatly increase the cost of music.

November 1951

Talking films

Our own film star is Mrs. Harry Legg. As winner of the net making competition in the Bath and West Show, she was invited to London to show her art in a talking film, her interrogator being Mr. Richard Dimbleby. Mrs. Legg confirms what others have said who have heard records of their voices, that one does not recognise one's own voice. 'The voice said what I had been saying,' said Mrs. Legg. 'So I suppose it was mine, but I should never have thought it.'

December 1951

Christmas in retrospect

We look back on Christmas, 1951, with feelings of pleasure and thankfulness. Parishes all over the country are saying that the religious observance of Christmas was better this time than for many years. A few comparisons shew how true this was of Loders. In 1931 our Christmas communicants numbered 70, and the collections in Christmas weeks were £4.5s. In 1941 the communicants were 57, and the collections £6. In 1951 the communicants were 110, and the collections £20. It was a heartening experience to have the church well filled four times in one week. The congregation at the midnight service was the biggest ever, and at matins on Christmas Day the church was packed really tight. So many other parishes are repeating a similar upward trend that these may be signs that the thoughts of the nation are returning to God. To those who have eyes to see, two world wars in half a century shew that modern man may have conquered the elements, but cannot conquer the evil in himself. Experience is also proving that the delightsome things of man's invention are a bad substitute for God in trying to satisfy the heart's deep longings.

January 1952

Village policeman and the Highwayman

The Choir collected £7.14s. by their carol-singing round the village. On their first night they received welcome hospitality at Upton and Matravers, and they ended their second night with refreshment and ghost stories round the big fireplace at the Vicarage. Here the village policeman [P.C. Edrich] delighted them with a recitation about a highwayman and an innkeeper's black-eyed daughter, which shewed that the Law is not entirely impervious to the nicer promptings of human nature. The Vicar's vampire story put some of the company to sleep. Or was it the mince pies?

January 1952

The late King George VI

London paid to George the Sixth the ceremonial honours due to a great King, but the simple tributes of the countryside were no less sincere and affectionate. If the dead know what is happening in this world, then the late King, whose heart was in the countryside, must have been touched by the way in which his country subjects flocked to the village churches to commend him to God. At Loders, Dottery and Askerswell the memorial services were on the Sunday following the King's death. There were large congregations at all three churches. On the day of the funeral some people went to church to keep the silence, and others joined in a short service in Loders Church in the evening. Loders ringers rang muffled peals. They 'turned in' the tenor bell, which, with the muffles, gave the music a rare and solemn effect. Much has been said, and written, of the late King. This, which was said of him by a native of the British West Indies, hits the proverbial nail on the head – 'In this humble and dutiful King we may see writ large the value and importance of the average man of decent instincts. . . . This sudden and sad event has focussed a spotlight on virtue, as opposed to brilliance and force and power.' We generally make the mistake of regarding the Archbishop of Canterbury as temporal head of the English Church, when actually it is the reigning Monarch. By living out the Christian faith so quietly, but so steadfastly, in 'the fierce light that beats upon the Throne', George the Sixth was a true disciple of his Master, and an example for which the English Church is grateful. He ranks with King Edward the Confessor as a Defender of the Faith.

March 1952

Misleading

A change has come over the farms of this neighbourhood since the war. The tired old sheds where the cows used to be milked have given place to spik and span milking parlours. The latest milking parlour is at a farm in Dottery. A lover of animals was pleased to see lace curtains at a window of this parlour. He took it to be part of the now general recognition that cows are ladies, presumably with a feminine weakness for lace, and an abhorrence of being milked by unshaven men. But his congratulations were lost on the puzzled farmer, who had put up the curtains as a precaution against witchcraft. That, at least, was what he implied when he said he was afraid of being overlooked.

March 1952

Letter for lying in state

Her Majesty Queen Elizabeth II promises to be as unsparing of herself as was her late father. With her own hand she has signed letters of thanks to all who did guard duty at the lying in state of King George VI. Sir Edward Le Breton has received one of these.

April 1952

The harassed Mr. Butler

Colonel Scott, now happily recovered from a sharp illness, shews a balance sheet for Loders Church for 1951 which the harassed Mr. Butler might well envy. A year of heavy expenditure ends with a balance on the right side, of £30. We have the good sense of the congregation to thank for this. They know that the expense of running a church goes on rising, and they give accordingly, without having to be asked. A happy consequence of this is that the subject of money is not often raised in our services, and they are the better for it.

June 1952

Generous New Zealand

Sir Edward Le Breton writes:- 'Would you kindly put in your monthly news sheet a note to the effect that another consignment of gift food from the generous New Zealanders has recently arrived, and the items allotted to this parish are 9 tins unsweetened milk, 6 tins cream, 11 tins minced beef, 12 tins sweets, and 23 packets pea and ham soup. I have been asked to collect these and distribute them. It is obvious that only a few of the 500 parishioners can benefit, and I propose as far as possible to give them out to people convalescing from illness, and needy pensioners. I hope this course will meet with the approval of the village.'

July 1952

Rationing

The gross takings of the fête were £133. 17s. 9d., expenses £22. 19s. 6d. and profit £110. 18s. 3d. The stalls made nearly £63, practically the same as in 1949 and 1950, when rationing was tight, and too much money was chasing too few goods. Doubtless it was a love of Loders Church that inspired such generous giving, and if we know Loders people, this will continue until church and organ are restored to a state of good repair.

September 1952

Outing without Corona

The juniors of Askerswell Choir began their outing in unpromising weather, but soon ran into sunshine, and apart from one shower when they were in the shelter of Cheddar Caves, they had a perfect day. They saw Glastonbury Abbey, and the swans on the moat of the Bishop's Palace at Wells which ring a bell when they are hungry. Having reached Wells a few minutes after eleven, they missed the hourly antics of the cathedral clock, and insisted on waiting till twelve. At Bath they joined a tour of the Roman baths, and saw the hot springs, which eject half a million gallons of water per week at a temperature of 120 degrees F. In the Pump-room they drank the warm mineral water favoured of ailing Kings, and said it wasn't a patch on Mrs. Norman's Corona, or even on the tea at Theobald's, where they refreshed themselves before the long journey home.

September 1952

To sea with Dr. Livingstone

A great grand-daughter of the Rev. Cox who was Rector of Askerswell in 1842 visited the church the other day. She lives in Australia. She said that Rev. Cox was chaplain of the ship on which Livingstone sailed to Africa.

September 1952

Autumn migration

The fall of the year is a recognised time for farms and farm cottages to change hands. But rarely are the changes on the scale now impending in Loders. The two biggest farms and some of their cottages are losing the present tenants, and so many non-farming residents have caught the urge to move that it approaches a mass migration. The houses to change hands are those occupied by Mr. Peckham, Mr. Edes, Mr. Hughes, Mrs. Edwards, Colonel Scott, Mr. Drake, Mr. Matthews, Mr. Shaw, Mr. Bishop, Mrs. Goldie, Mr. Allsop, Mr. Harwood, and Mrs. Lenthall. Other moves are being considered. Added to those that have taken place fairly recently, they make a large number for a small village. Dottery presents a striking contrast. Its inhabitants change but rarely. Mrs. Rolleston's is the only move at present contemplated, and hers is back to America. Why does nobody (except a few old established families) stay long in Loders, and why does everybody stay in Dottery? Is the atmosphere of Dottery pleasant, and are the people there fond of each other? We doubt the truth of the suggestion that they are too satisfied with the Blue Ball to leave it, estimable as that hostelry is.

October 1952

Lynmouth Relief Fund

Loders W.I. raised nearly £30 for this fund by a whist drive and stall. The collection made by Mrs. Allsop in Uploders produced £14. 8s., and Askerswell Community Club is running a whist drive for the same object.

October 1952

Great War trench martyr

October has left a trail of bereavement in its wake, and our sympathy is with those chiefly concerned. Mr. David Symes, who had carried on a market gardening business near the Old Mill in Loders, died in Allington, and was buried at Loders cemetery, very near the plot of ground on which he had done his life's work. Mr. Sidney Collier-Marsh, who died following an accident in Bridport, was also of Loders stock. He was a martyr to an infection of the foot acquired in the trenches of France during the Great War. Mrs. Chignell, of Spyway, died under an operation. She was one who could love the seclusion of her own home, and yet be intensely interested in the doings of the parish. To chat with her was refreshment, and her serenity and sense of humour were with her to the end. The mother of Mrs. Streatfield, Lady Davies, died rather suddenly in London. Her ashes reposed for one night in Loders Church on their way to the family burying place.

November 1952

Loders Coronation plans

At a recent meeting of the Committee, the Secretary reported that the skittling for a pig had produced £26.10. The sum in hand is now almost £100. To enable people to have their fill of Coronation broadcasting, the fancy dress procession from Matravers to the Court will not begin unitl 3.30 p.m., and the sports will follow the tea instead of preceding it. The sports will give scope to both sexes and most ages, and also to the age-old rivalry between Loders and Uploders, one of which will have the satisfaction of pulling the other through the river. Parish councillors who do not shine in the dialectical battles of the council chambers may be revenged on their more eloquent opponents by attaching themselves to the opposite end of the rope, for eloquence and brawn seldom go together. The Coronation Committee had one matter to settle which might have caused Solomon to think. A Loders inn and an Uploders inn each expressed willingness to cater for thirst at the evening celebrations in the Hut. The Committee, anxious to avoid splitting the parish by shewing a preference for either, informed the

worthy landlords that they were quite capable of settling
between themselves which should do it. But the landlords were
not to be had. They insisted on a decision from the
Committee. Thereupon the Committee submitted the thorny
question to the gods. An Uploders gentleman spun a coin, a
Loders gentleman said, 'Heads', and so the coin decreed that
the Uploders inn should do the job. But ancient rivals may not
be placated thus easily. The name of the Uploders gentleman
who spun the coin has leaked out, and Loders is deeply suspi-
cious. The committee meeting ended with an appeal from Mr.
Wilfred Crabb for inflammable material for the bonfire which
he and the other parish councillors are organising. It was news
to the rest of the committee that the councillors ever lacked
inflammable matter.

May 1953

In memoriam

Muffled peals in memory of the late Queen Mary were rung
at Loders on the day of her funeral.

May 1953

The centre of gravity

Loders Coronation began with a royal salute from the belfry
which was repeated at intervals through the day. An appreciable
congregation met in church for prayers, and a move was then
made for the television sets, of which wealthy Uploders has
three, and Loders one. Mr. Rice-Oxley had converted his small
drawing room into a theatre seating nearly forty. The afternoon
fancy dress procession from Matravers had to take cover from
the rain during the judging, but its progress to the Court was in
warm sunshine, and parishioners at their doors and windows
cheered it on. The young competitors who formed the procession were already in good spirits (having all received prizes of
some sort) when they reached the lawn of Loders Court, and
their enthusiasm mounted when they saw tables laden with good
things to eat, and a large cake wearing a sugar crown. Dottery
were already there. A company of about 300 sat down to tea,
and having to duck beneath the tables during a shower only

added to the fun. The sports which followed were highly amusing, and the climax was a tug-o'-war between Loders and Dottery. (The Uploders team had decided to avoid defeat by not competing.) As there was a good chance of the teams getting pneumonia without pulling across the stream, they pulled on the grass, and Loders managed to win a tough fight. The festivities then moved to the Hut, whose interior had been transformed by red, white and blue hangings, and whose exterior, like Westminster Abbey, had been fitted with an Annexe, rudely contrived of iron bars and tarpaulin, but delicately furnished with alcoholic comforts, and presided over by the genial landlord of the Crown. The party was true to form. Fathers found their centre of gravity in the Annexe; mothers, children and youths enjoyed the games and dances in the Hut. At nine o'clock the Queen's speech brought everybody into the Hut, winkling the most tenacious maltworms out of the Annexe, and Mrs. Harry Legg took this opportunity of unloading on the united company a vast store of ham sandwiches and cakes. The day concluded with a bonfire on Knowle Hill, and fireworks on the bank outside the Hut. These were let off by Mr. Charlie Gale and Mr. Wilfred Crabb with fine disregard for personal safety. When a rocket exploded before taking off, the crowd were relieved to see the living forms of the operators emerge unhurt, and still clothed, from the smoke. The crowd also admired the heroism with which Mr. Gale diverted the aim of a high powered and already fizzing rocket from Mr. Randall's strawrick to the sky. Old people and invalids who were not able to join in the celebrations received souvenir tins of tea or biscuits, and the children have yet to be treated to the Coronation film when it visits Bridport.

June 1953

Royal mementoes

Coronation mugs, the gift of Sir Edward and Lady Le Breton, were distributed on the lawn of Loders Court by their grandson, Master Edward Laskey, lately home from New York.

June 1953

Coronation from Sarum

The Diocesan Service of Thanksgiving for the Coronation took place as planned at Old Sarum, and is already a treasured memory of the thousands who took part in it. Such is our English weather that the organisers must have been on tenterhooks right till the time that the great service began. Heavy rain had fallen in the morning, and the afternoon was palled over by a mist which could not decide whether to condense or evaporate. But the organisers were men of faith, and their gamble on an open air service rather than on one in the cathedral was blest by a perfect evening. Some of our readers may be unaware that Old Sarum is a vast mound two miles north of Salisbury. It is a 'windswept height', chosen the site of the first city of Salisbury because it could be easily defended. In process of time the inhabitants of Old Sarum decided that draughts were the worst enemy of all, so they built another city, the present Salisbury, near the river Avon. But Old Sarum still contains the ruins of the Castle, and the site of the first cathedral. So it was to Old Sarum that a multitude of worshippers from the far-flung diocese of Salisbury came on the evening of July 1st to identify themselves with the Queen's act of self-dedication to God in the Coronation.

July 1953

Elijah comes to Old Sarum

The scene was vaguely reminiscent of Elijah's contest with Baal on Mount Carmel. The skylarks, who normally have the hilltop to themselves, rose up in a frightened chorus from beneath the foot of the first intruder, who saw coaches, cars and pedestrians converging on them from all points of the compass. Soon the old cathedral and its surrounds was peopled by a congregation the largest it had ever known, and a long procession of white robed choristers, clergy in the colourful hoods of their degrees, and three mitred bishops, moved down the open nave to an altar, high and lifted up. When the Bishop of Salisbury, Dr. Anderson, turned west to face the congregation and begin the service, a blue clearing broke in the clouds above, the sun came out gloriously, and the evening was perfect. In moments of religious fervour, the sublime and the ridiculous may blend unobtrusively. The ancient clergyman in cassock, surplice, hood, and trilby hat (which he had forgotten to remove) was no longer an oddity, and the resplendent generals of Southern Command seated in the transepts were doubtless thinking it was meet and right that the Air Force wallahs should be making the mess they were of the amplifying. Our Dottery churchwardens raised an eyebrow when they found the collection being taken by two gentlemen with sacks, and our Vicar permitted himself to observe that of faith these gentlemen might have none, their charity might even be in doubt, but their hope never.

July 1953

Mrs. Lenthall gets her way

A coachload of thirty-one persons from our three parishes attended the Old Sarum service. But they had first made a day of it by visiting Stourhead, and viewing the treasurers of Longleat House. They partook of a picnic lunch at Heaven's Gate, the beauty spot overlooking Longleat, where Bishop Ken wrote 'Glory to thee, my God, this night', and other famous hymns. Here was a wooden seat, and when the announcement was made that the old people might have the first refusal of it, there were suddenly no old people. Mrs. Lenthall, the head of our Mothers' Union, has marked this phenomenon, and turned it to good use, for when she wanted ALL the Mothers' Union to help in spring cleaning, the church, she appealed to the younger ones only – and got everybody.

July 1953

CHAPTER 3

The church's year

Muscular Christianity

With the Book of Common Prayer behind him and before him and largely known off by heart, the Vicar inherited the central traditions of the Church of England. He knew much of Hymns Ancient and Modern off by heart, with their numbers at his fingertips to alert the organist and congregation. He could not abide 'Abide with me', not for footballing reasons, but because it advocated a passive, fatalistic religion of which he did not approve. Though by his own definition originally 'a near-papist', (see page 107), he responded sympathetically to the needs of his flock and to the Protestant customs of his three Dorset churches. In fact, he was a rural ecumenicalist in disguise. Plough Sunday and Harvest were as prominent as Easter, and times of service had to synchronize with the demands of milking. He encouraged music and bells and flowers but, after the altar, the pulpit was his central stand. He delivered faultless, fifteen-minute sermons without a note, keeping the attention of his congregation in a tight grip. Scriptural explanations were mixed with lively anecdotes from experience or from that week's paper. All was in his memory, apart from on the odd scrap of paper with a quote. The sermons were timed meticulously on his watch, as he 'sermonized' with the dog, round the village lanes. He would sometimes preach two or three different sermons on the same day. His nickname at Kelham was 'Timon' (with, we hope, no negative implications). His sermons were made substantial by his unshakeable convictions, his deep theological training, his wide interest in science and current affairs, his knowledge of his congregation and his capacity to entertain. There are no sermons in these extracts from the *Parish Notes*, unfortunately. Only a couple are retained in his script or on tape. But his Christianity and humanity are given ample demonstration here. The *Parish Notes were* his secular arm.

He always brought humour to things religious, even to funerals and baptisms. At one funeral, well before the time of guitars in the chancel, he got the congregation to clap the memory of a well-lived, well-loved old colonel. One of the things left out of this abridgement is the simple list of the services of the month – except for Easter 1952 which appears on page 72. That one example is a reminder of the intensity of his ministry, racing across the nine miles of his parish to get to the next communion on time. He managed ten services in three churches during one day, with several sermons. He built up the traditions of Christmas services; he experimented successfully with evensong (though sometimes the singing disappointed his sense of high standards); he tried hard to make St. Mary Magdalene's Day (July 22nd) a proud Patronal Day. He strove to revive the customs of the Village Feast at the same time.

His congregation over the years was enormous, via the pulpit, the *Parish Notes* and the pub. His care for the fabric of the churches was part of his very practical, down-to-earth mission. He did not mind stooping to cut the grass, and even to reposition recumbent tomb-stones when necessary. Visiting the sick at home and in hospital, and talking to all newcomers, Christian or otherwise, was how he spread the Word. He also visited the well and extended his ministry into their frontroom where he gleaned parish news by the by.

Whilst pious, and even saintly sometimes, his muscular Christianity was marked by wit and generosity of spirit (except when engaged in a discussion where he felt he had the one and only answer). His bishops were men of muscle too: Bishop Lunt of Salisbury was awarded the MC; Dr Anderson had the unusual distinction of having been a sergeant in the Army, having won the DSO in the Navy, and having obtained a pilot's certificate in the RAF before being ordained (see page 158). Bishop Pike of Sherborne, his bishop later in his ministry, had served as an Irish Rugby Union International. But the Vicar's voice, wherever it was heard, was distinct without being military, and unforgettably soft and serious when leading the Holy Communion. A traditionalist at heart, his training with the Missionary Society in Bristol made him truly ecumenical in practice, preaching unity without union. Chaucer (see pages 200–1) would have been proud of him.

Tribute by a parishioner

'The crowning glory was his ability in his sermons to make his congregation sit up and take notice, so that they digested his theological thoughts without realizing it.'

Loders Church

When the Vicar attended his first meeting of the Bridport Ruri-Decanal Chapter, he was told by one clerical brother after another that they envied him his lovely church. In age and beauty, the priory church of Loders has no equal in the Bridport Deanery. It is high time that the parish set aside one Sunday of the year on which to thank God for its church. Many parishes, with less to be thankful for, do this. Therefore we shall keep Sunday, July 25th, as our Dedication Festival. It is the Sunday nearest the feast day of our patron saint, Mary Magdalene. There will be Holy Communion at 8, Matins at 11, Children's Service at 2.30, and Evensong at 6.30. It is hoped that the ladies who decorate will make the church look its best, and that the congregation at Evensong may be as big as that on Rogation Sunday.

July 1948

Sunday School Outing

By a big majority, the children voted Bournemouth for their Outing. Obviously, the amount of time a modern child has to spend in buses has not quelled the youthful instinct for getting as far afield as possible. We hope that many parents and friends will join the Outing and share responsibility for the children.

August 1948

Walls have ears

Some good folk visit Dottery Church on Sunday afternoons to tend graves. Although there are many signs of it, they seem unaware that a service is going on inside the church. The walls of Dottery Church are thin. We inside try to be polite, and turn a deaf ear to conversation not intended for us, but it is difficult. When a sermon has to compete for the congregation's attention with a private heart-to-heart talk on the other side of the tin, what chance has the sermon?

August 1948

Church upkeep

The holes in the ceilings of Ladye Chapel and the Porch have
been skilfully repaired, but the cost, nearly £26, has left a hole
in the Repair Fund. There is a widespread idea that because
the Church of England is the national church, all parish
churches, and more so cathedrals, are maintained out of rates
or taxes. Actually, the money has to be found by the people
who use the church. The State contributes nothing.

August 1948

Day-tripping

The Sunday School Outing to Bournemouth was delayed an
hour in starting, while a forty-seater coach was being fetched,
to cope with the unexpectedly large company of trippers. The
fine weather had decided many waverers at the last minute, and
the Vicar had taken a chance which did not come off – he had
not cycled to Dottery the previous evening and checked their
final numbers. Fortunately for him, people are used to inconvenience these days, and this seemed but a trifle to the trippers.
The day was a happy one. The party numbered over 120, and
their ages ranged from a few months to well over 80 years. It
was much regretted that the Elliott family, staunchest supporters of the Sunday School, could not join the outing. Mary had
gone down with chickenpox only three days previously.

September 1948

Keeping money in the parish

'I'm glad the money is for the school. Too much goes out of
the parish.' Words to this effect were on several Loders lips at
the time of the fête. They show *how* ill-informed the parish is
on its financial affairs. This may not be the fault of the parish.
The story told by the minute book is that Loders gives much
to its own parish church, but very little to the Church outside
the parish. Yet the Church outside the Parish has been
subscribing about £100 year, for many years, to the maintenance of the church in Loders. The combined tithe of Loders
and Dottery is worth only £210 year. Not even a Vicar could
live on that. Last year other parishes subscribed about £150 to

the maintenance of Loders Vicar and Vicarage. If other parishes took the line that no money was to go outside, there would be no resident vicar in Loders.

September 1948

Service wage

Miss Welstead and her small team of collectors have done well in raising £20. 4s. 8d. for the Bishop's Appeal in the quarter just ended. This included several generous donations, among them one of £5. The Vicar is heartened by this evidence that there are far-seeing people in the parish. Without parsons there can be no Church. At a time when the population of Britain is the highest ever, the number of the clergy is the lowest ever – last year 208 were ordained, as against 590 in 1938. Much of the Bishop's Appeal money goes towards the cost (at least £1,000 per head) of training the 1,500 Servicemen who have been accepted for the sacred ministry. Bear in mind the financial sacrifice these men are making! During their three years' training they earn nothing, and when they qualify, theirs will be a wage which is the joke of the other learned professions.

October 1948

Remembrance Sunday

November is the solemn month of the year. Within it occurs the fall of the leaves, the feast of All Hallows, All Souls' day, and the remembrance of those who fell in the two world wars. November 7th is Remembrance Sunday. We hope that Loders will make a big day of it. The new memorial tablet which the Parish Council is adding to the existing memorial, should be ready for dedication on that day. The chief service will be at 10.45 a.m. so as to include the Two Minutes' Silence. Will the parish organisations kindly regard this as an official invitation to attend – Parish Council, British Legion, Oddfellows, Discussion Club, Young Farmers, Agricultural Workers' Union, Mothers' Union and Women's Institute? The collection will be for Earl Haig's Fund. At Dottery, the Remembrance Service will be at 6.30.

November 1948

Christmas presents

The Sunday School children hope that you will not buy your
Christmas presents before you have been to the little sale they
are to hold in the Vicarage early in December. It is a job of
work they are doing for the Church overseas. Incidentally they
want to recover the good name of Loders. Last year we
contributed only 30/- to missionary work, and were at the
bottom of the list for the whole diocese. Hamlets with a
quarter of our population beat us hands down. To go and teach
all nations is the first of Our Lord's marching orders to
Christians, and Loders has no valid excuse for disobeying.
Every parish has its difficulties, and we have less than most.
To the person who sees no good in missions, the answer is that
in this he is at variance with the Almighty, whose opinion is
at least as good as his.

November 1948

The moral state of the nation

Mrs. Pritchard and Mrs. Paul became members of the
Mothers' Union at an enroling service held recently in Loders
Church. The M.U. stands for the integrity of home life, and
never, since the collapse of the Roman Empire, was this in
more danger than it is today. Women who are not mothers, but
who agree with the M.U. ideals, may become Associates.

November 1948

War dead

Remembrance Sunday was another satisfying day. The deep
throated bells of Loders, half-muffled, called the village to
honour its war dead, and the church filled right up for the
service. Poppies were to the fore – a wreath on the memorial,
and three upright crosses in the chancel. The new memorial,
commissioned by the Parish Council, was not ready, but the
congregation bore the disappointment with good grace. The
singing of favourites like 'Jerusalem' and 'Valiant Hearts' was
emphatic, and the Choir's anthem exactly suited the occasion.
It was pleasing to have the churchyard thronged with people

after service, and the bells pealing overhead. God's house had again become a focus of interest, and the ancient place seemed happy.

December 1948

Evensong

The congregation at the fortnightly evensong is steadily increasing, and reached the fifties in November. There is a cosy, restful feeling about this service, and the singing is hearty. Uploders is very loyal in its support.

December 1948

The Christmas touch

The midnight service on Christmas Eve promises to be a popular institution. The body of the church was comfortably full. There was no light, except from the two candles on the altar, and from the fairy lamps on the tree in the chancel, which gave the Christmas touch.

January 1949

Returning to their roots

Many old faces of relations home for Christmas appeared at morning service on Christmas Day. This was a memorable service. The children sang carols round the lighted Christmas tree, and received from Mrs. Welstead packets of sweets given by our branch of the Mothers' Union. Prayer books were presented to Margaret & Reginald Drake, and a book token to Beryl Tilley, for unbroken Sunday School attendance. The congregation filled the church.

January 1949

The least popular season

Lent begins on March 2nd. It is the least popular season of the Church's year, and so we should be careful to do it justice. A custom cannot survive for the best part of two thousand years, as Lent has done, without good reason, and the virtue of Lent is that it gives us an annual reminder that we are sinners, and that we ought to do something about it while our limited opportunity lasts. The Vicar asked the Church Council whether the parish would be likely to support a weekday service in Lent. The Council thought that a weekday service would be so poorly attended as to be not worthwhile. Having lived here longer than the Vicar, the Council should know the parish better than he, and he bows to the Council's opinion, hoping that a Lenten weekday service may become, one day, an established thing. Meanwhile, we can make Lent a reality by attending Holy Communion more often. It is a personal meeting with Our Lord, transcending every other service. One wishes that our young people could have the affection of the older people for it. Most of these who were confirmed last Whitsun have failed their rule of monthly Communion, which was never a very ambitious one, and some let even the great festivals go by. The plea is made that everybody is busy, or tired, yet our hours of work are shorter and our hours of leisure are longer, very considerably, than those of any generation before us.

At matins during Lent the sermons will be on the prophet Jonah, and at evensong, on the prophet Amos. These prophets are too relevant to our times to be contained in single sermons. The Vicar relies on regular attendance in Lent to make these serial sermons effective.

February 1949

The church seating

When people attend the same meeting frequently, they tend to make for the same seat each time. We all have our own preferences, and the seat we habitually use tends to be regarded, both by ourselves and by others, as one to which we have a right. This tendency shows itself quite naturally in church, and when church attendance is small it gives rise to no difficulties, but when the weather is kind, our Sunday morning congregations are large, and contain a big proportion of non-parishioners. These non-parishioners are very welcome, but many of them do not practise the etiquette of asking the verger where to sit when they are in a church which is not their own, and the consequence is that regular parishioners sometimes find their favourite seats occupied. This matter was raised at the recent meeting of the Church Council. The Council sympathised with the regular worshippers, and the churchwardens promised to do what they could to see that these situations did not arise, but the Council felt strongly that it was the first duty of the church to make all visitors welcome. We can be certain that Jesus would give up his seat to a stranger, even if the stranger had disregarded the proprieties, and would rejoice that there was another guest in His Father's house. As a matter of interest, seating is something in which the churchwarden is all powerful. According to Dak's 'Law of the Parish Church', he allots all ordinary sittings, and is answerable neither to the Church Council, nor to the incumbent, but to the Bishop only. All parishioners have a right to a seat in their parish church when seats enough are available, and they have a right to their allotted seat if they are in it when the five minute bell begins. Non-parishioners have no legal rights in a parish church. Yet as guests, and fellow Christians, their claims are above everything.

February 1949

The centurion's boots

It is good for parsons to have their sermons pulled to bits and chewed over. Besides, any shred of evidence that somebody was awake and listening, is to be hailed with delight. The nice people do their chewing with the parson, enabling him to explain himself better, and perhaps 'larning him' a thing or two. It is curious that so many people should have told the Vicar of their surprise at hearing from the pulpit that Roman centurions wore hobnailed boots, and not sandals. He gave as his authority the Roman Poet Juvenal, who pokes fun at centurions' hobnailed boots in his Satires (XVI. 14, 24). The Vicar has since learned that a member of the congregation once saw and handled, in the old London Museum, a Roman boot, dug out of the London clay.

March 1949

Corporate Communion

Lady Day, March 25, is on Friday this year. The Mothers'
Union will make their Corporate Communion at 10 o'clock
that day, in place of the normal monthly meeting.

March 1949

Holiday or Holy Day?

Good Friday is the dying day of Our Lord. If He means
anything to us, we shall be thinking in love and wonder of what
He did for us on that day. Calvary will be repeated. There will
be a handful of sympathisers at the foot of the Cross, and there
will be a multitude of holidaymakers, on the roads and at the
seaside, callously indifferent to the Man of Sorrows, and cruci-
fying the Son of God afresh. Holy Scripture teaches that the

way of multitudes is the way to perdition. It was not the priests nor Pontius Pilate who signed His death warrant, but the multitudes, for they alone could have saved Him. In Loders, farm work will have to continue on Good Friday. As you go about the farm, or bend over your garden, think of Calvary, and in the evening come to the 8 o'clock service in your old parish church, where the Good Friday watch has been kept for 800 years and more.

April 1949

Mothers' Union to Sherborne Abbey

'When that April with his showers sweet
The drought of March hath pierced unto the root ....
Then longen folk to goon on pilgrimages.'

(Chaucer)

The spring weather awakened the urge to pilgrimage in our Mothers' Union and on the gorgeous afternoon of Lady Day they joined a great concourse of Dorset mothers at a service in Sherborne Abbey. The Secretary, Mrs. Lenthall, had made the arrangements with her usual thoroughness. Our mothers were the guests at tea of their Enroling Member, Mrs. Welstead, and the tea alone was worth the pilgrimage. Loders is very near the Bishop of Sherborne's idea of paradise [Victor Joseph Key]. He said, after the Abbey service, that he still hoped to retire to Loders! But for the unexpected illness of a sister, he and his family would have spent their last summer holiday in Loders Vicarage.

April 1949

Easter in retrospect

Easter, 1949, was the ideal Easter, and the happiest that some of us can remember. We made our way to early Communion in sunshine that had the warmth of summer, while the leaves, the flowers, and the song of the birds, had the freshness of spring. There was just enough breeze to stir the flag of St George on the tower battlements, and the air vibrated with the Easter bells. The old sanctuary of Loders had been turned into a dream of

beauty by the loving hands of women and children. The altar
was a bank of arum lilies, blackthorn and narcissi, and not a
niche nor cranny of the church was without its flowers. The
throng of communicants included Miss Doreen Watts, who used
to live in Loders, and still loves it, but is now in exile in Shipton
Gorge, whence her father motored her early. At Matins the
church was full. This was a memorable service. The monks of
Loders Priory, and an unseen host of bygone worshippers
seemed to be lending their voices to the triumphant shouts of
Easter. It was pleasing to note how some hard working farming
families came to church in relays, different members to each
service, so as to leave somebody on duty at home. Yet, happy
as the day was, it had its tinge of sadness. Some of God's family,
who might have been in their Father's House on this greatest of
days, were not there, and He must have missed them.

May 1949

Easter offering

The Vicar says, 'Thank you very much indeed' for the contributions made towards his stipend on Easter Day. They reached
the useful sum of £17. 14s. 0d. One Easter offering came from
a parishioner in hospital, another from the Infirmary, and
another from a grievous sick bed. Remembrance made in
circumstances like these is precious indeed.

May 1949

Farmers in force

'Plough' Sunday will be kept on May 22nd. We hope to have
a service at 6.30 p.m., on the same lines as last year, when
the farming community attended in force, and the church was
crowded.

June 1949

Still true?

An old letter in the parish chest that came to light the other
day, contains this sentence: 'Loders used to be a very troublesome parish indeed, and Vicars used to come and go rather
frequently'.

August 1949

Paying our share

Our quota to the Diocesan Central Fund has just been increased from £16 to £21. There have been other increases in the running expenses of the church, which are met out of church collections, and we look like ending the year with a deficit. However, Central Funds are letting us down very very lightly in requiring only a £21 quota from Loders. Our neighbour, Walditch, with a quarter of our population, pays £17, and does not receive £150 grant from central funds, as we do.

August 1949

The fortnightly evensong

The Vicar's recent announcement that the fortnightly evensong in Loders would henceforth have to be said, because of lack of congregation to sing it properly, has generated a surprising storm of resentment in the village. The tiny knot of regular worshippers, almost to a man, has accepted the decision with the sorrow with which it was made, a sorrow tempered with understanding. The most grievous hurt seems to have been suffered by those who never come. 'Absence makes the heart grow fonder', perhaps? There is a good case for making an effort to continue the sung service. The few at night are as important as the many in the morning, and have an equal right to hymn and sermon, but God has his rights too. Public worship must not be depressing, and that is what our evensong had become. Many people, at different times, have joined us, but have not come again. The rows of empty pews, mutely telling how the multitudes have fallen away from the worship of God, and the brave efforts of a few scattered souls to sing chants they do not know, leave the casual worshipper with the impression that God is dead. Then preaching is not as easy as it looks. Demosthenes was one of those giants of oratory who could declaim as effectively to the sea as to the Athenian senate. But we are not all Demosthenes. At the end of a heavy day, when perhaps he has preached three different sermons already, a vicar may come with his fourth to a nigh empty church, and be so disheartened that he cannot concentrate on the sermon. If the sermon is not written out, he is wiser to leave the pulpit alone.

There is a saying, 'It is no use aiming high if you haven't any ammunition.' As yet, we haven't the ammunition for a sung evensong. So the plan is, to say it for the time being. The organist will stand by. If enough people come, we may be able to sing hymns, and go on to simple chants. It would be fine to have an evening congregation which could sing the office without leadership.

September 1949

Paean

Sometimes Loders people are exasperating beyond words. At Harvest they were very lovable. They made the Festival exactly what it was meant to be, and created a memory which will feed the flickering flame of hope when hope has nothing else to feed upon. In the dark days of winter we shall remember the golden brightness of the church on Harvest morning. Our minds' eye will see the sheaves, the autumn blooms, the nesting eggs, and the heavenly pink of the belladonna lilies in the chancel. Our noses may again catch the homely scent of apples, and our ears will never quite have lost the notes of the Harvest anthem. Whenever the size of the congregation suggests that Loders could not care less about God, we shall hug to our hearts the recollection that on Harvest Sunday the church was filled twice in one day, and shall see again the crowd of worshippers having a last word with each other in the churchyard before going home, and trying to make themselves heard above the frolicking of the bells.

October 1949

Dropping a brick

Taxi-driver, to lady passenger: 'I've no time for parsons. They only work one day a week. 'Ave you?'
Passenger: 'Well, I happen to be the wife of one. . . .'

December 1949

Another successful experiment

On the Sunday evening after Christmas we tried out the Service of the Nine Lessons, and it was well received. A large congregation sat and watched the lighted Christmas tree, and listened to the choir singing old carols, such as 'I saw three ships', 'God rest you merry', and 'The Holly and the Ivy'. Each of the nine lessons should have been read by a parishioner representing a part of the parochial organisation, but only two could be induced to lift up their voices in public. The prevailing shyness may wear off by next year. It was good to have the Dottery congregation in their mother church for this service, and to see them round the Vicarage fire with cups of tea afterwards. Their feeling for Mr. Charlie Gale was warm, for he had hurried back from an emergency job to be their coachman.

February 1950

Spring cleaning

When wives begin to plan this, long-suffering husbands protest that the annual disturbance would be unnecessary if the routine cleaning had been done properly. To which wives retort that the best ordered house is better after spring cleaning. So it is with Lent. Nobody likes this annual disturbance, but it is good for us, and is more than ever necessary now, when we are slack in the routine duty of Sunday worship. We are living in a house whose windows are cobwebbed over, and so coated with dirt that the sunshine of God's Spirit cannot get in. We make for ourselves an artificial light, and give our energy to the moth-eaten interests of making money to secure our future, or of pandering to the flesh which we know is only dust. Lent means cleaning our windows, seeing the brightness of the love of God all round us, seeing our own dinginess, and finally throwing open our windows to God's influence. On Thursday afternoons in Lent at three o'clock, we shall study one of the prophets; on alternate Sunday evenings in Lent the sermon will be by the Vicar of Bradpole. A new voice from the pulpit should be welcome.

February 1950

Communicants rally

It is pleasing to report an increased number of communicants at the 8 o'clock service. They had thinned out in January and early February. It must hurt Our Lord to be there waiting in vain to meet His people in His own service.

March 1950

Present-giving in church

On Mothering Sunday our children took to their service presents they had made for their mothers, and bunches of flowers they had collected for old people and invalids. The presents were put on a table in the chancel, and the flowers were laid at the altar. The mothers, determined not to disappoint their children, came to church in strength, bringing other grown-ups with them, and in the course of a pretty service the children had the satisfaction of seeing their mothers called up to the chancel by the Vicar to received the presents the children had made. After service, the children collected the flowers from the altar, and went in a body from end to end of the village handing out their posies. Faces appeared at many doors and windows, and sometimes the mothering was applauded.

April 1950

Holy Week and Easter

We have come to the most sacred season in the Church's year. To our modern minds it seems a pity that Jesus did not keep a diary (as did Julius Caesar), giving us his own thoughts about the Passion. But it is his will that we should be content with the account in the Gospels. These tell us what happened to Jesus on each day of Holy Week. The language is restrained and unemotional, but it goes right to the hearts of those who let it touch their imagination. The Last Supper was two thousand years ago. It was two thousand years ago when the Cross was reared on Calvary. But what are two thousand years beside the millions of years of the earth's existence? Good Friday seems like yesterday. The diary of Holy Week has been left to us so that we may live through that week, and have our eyes so opened to the badness of our sins, that we crucify them on Good Friday, and rise to a new life of goodness on Easter Day.

April 1950

Milking Easter

Our Mother Church of England is not dictatorial about attendance at Holy Communion. Like Our Lord, she leaves it to the individual conscience. But she does ask specifically that Easter be one of the days on which Communion is made, and her loyal sons and daughters will not let her ask in vain. Milking is a problem for some would-be communicants, but the services at 7 a.m. and 11.45 a.m. should give them an opportunity.

April 1950

Church business

The Easter Vestry and Annual Church Meeting is open to the whole village, and is an important event. The parishioners receive from the retiring church council a balance sheet and an account of their year's stewardship. Churchwardens and sidesmen are then appointed, and a church council elected. Attendance in the two years previous to this has been excellent, and we hope it will be maintained. This year the meeting is on the Wednesday in Easter week, at the School, at 7.30 p.m.

April 1950

Tractors for ploughs?

The Farm Service in Loders Church on Rogation Sunday has become a popular institution. This year it will be on May 14th at 6.30 p.m. The farmer who suggested that it would be more in keeping with the times to have a tractor in the chancel, instead of our ancient plough, did not say how we were to get the tractor in.

May 1950

Ultra-Protestants

Loders Church looked rather gay in Lent. Loders Court kept the alter beautiful with flowers, Uploders Place sent a lovely cluster of pot plants for the base of the chancel arch, the Lady's Chapel and the War Memorial were specially attractive and somebody put pots of primroses round the font. A person with a sense of liturgical propriety might well have thought that we were ultra-protestants, brazenly defying the tradition of no flowers in Lent. But that is not so. It just happened that way. Our Lord is certain to have been pleased with these offerings and they gave the Church an air of being loved.

May 1950

The churchyard

Mr. Gray, the poet, was inspired by the peace of a country churchyard to write his immortal Elegy. We wonder whether that same churchyard spelt peace and inspiration to the Vicar of Stoke Poges, who was responsible for its good order. In these days, the difficulty of getting labour, even at a high price, makes churchyards and cemeteries the desperation of those who have the care of them. The Parish Council are now forced to make a levy of £4 on each new grave in Loders cemetry to meet the maintenance charges. This is additional to the other funeral expenses. In Loders churchyard there is no maintenance charge of any kind, and people who have graves there are entirely responsible for clipping them. This is done regularly by some. We hope that in future it will be done by all. We are very grateful to Mr. Elliott, of Yondover, for undertaking our scything on reasonable terms. He might be willing to make an arrangement with people who would like him to clip their graves.

May 1950

Junior choir

The Choir has produced an offspring. Some half dozen young girls, with nice voices, turn out for practice before the main choir practice, and sit in front of the choir on Sundays, when they are most useful. They are styled 'The Junior Choir'.

June 1950

Bringing them to church

It is noticeable how often people who have left their home parish come back to the church and point out the pew where they and their wives used to sit when they were courting. The church is interwoven with the romances of a great number of today's steadfast married couples. Nothing could be better than this. Now it is not so common for courting couples to be seen in church. Indeed, the present experience of parsons is to miss their staunch young people from the accustomed pew, to miss them again the following Sunday, to think that they must be ill, and to find that they are courting. We note that some of our staunch young ladies bring their young men to church. We are delighted to have them, and are grateful for the example.

July 1950

Farewell to summer

The stream of summer visitors to Loders Church has now thinned to a trickle, and we miss them. In July and August Scouts camping in the park swelled the morning congregations. Sometimes the church was so full of visitors that Loders faces had to be looked for. Eyes new to Loders are captivated by the beauty of the church and its approach, and strangers cannot think why the villagers do not flock to it. Several families holidaying at West Bay did all their worshipping in our church, one such family attending at 8 and 11 each Sunday for three weeks. Another family came specially from Bournemouth for evensong, having previously sent the Vicar a list of their favourite hymns, in the hope that some might be included that evening! It is a mercy for us that our church is old and attractive and not young and ugly. The collections from visitors keep our finances solvent, and it is visitors who supply our church with worshippers.

October 1950

Honouring the war dead

Remembrance Sunday, when we honour the dead of the two great wars, falls on November 12th this year. Our big service will be at 11 o'clock, instead of the usual 10.45. The earlier time seems just a bit too early for those who have work to do before Sunday morning church. The Dottery remembrance service will be at 6.30 p.m. At both services the collections will be for Earl Haig's Fund. Mr. J.C. Shoobridge, local secretary of the British Legion, has asked us to give generously. His account of what is done with the Poppy Day money makes interesting reading. Poppy Day helps to provide a weekly allowance for 3,336 permanently disabled ex-Servicemen, homes for nearly 4,000 convalescents, nearly £4,000 for homes for paralysed men, and over £800,000 for the benevolent department. Last year it even granted £3,000 to 25 Ex-Servicemen who are training for Ordination.

November 1950

Saint Pumpkin

Marrows and pumpkins were conspicuous in the decoration scheme for Loders Harvest Festival. We would not care to estimate the weight of the giant green marrow that came from the Court. Captain Welstead's pumpkin was so big that it lent credibility to the alleged origin of Cinderella's coach. One of Mr. Stevens' two pumpkins was inscribed 'Be thankful', and the other 'Harvest Festiful'. (Only one person commented on the originality of Mr. Stevens' spelling.) A bunch of strawberries, and not the preacher, was the focus of the congregation's attention to the pulpit. Miss Hinks had sent these. There were also eggs in abundance, and honey and preserves. The *pièce de résistance* was the five barley loaves and the two small fishes on a dish, done in bread by Mr. Caddy. If the tenth commandment was broken during the service, the breakers should be the small poultry-keepers in the congregation, who were expected to think of God in full view of two bags of corn adorning the chancel arch. Mr. Lenthall will have something to answer for – but not to the Parish Clerk and the Vicar, who keep a hen or two. Seeing that several neighbouring parishes were keeping Harvest on the same day, our congregations were surprisingly large. They greatly enjoyed the music of Mr. Bill Tiltman and the choir. Miss V. Legg was the soloist in the anthem. The total Harvest collection for Loders parish (which includes Dottery, of course) was £15.

November 1950

A doctor in the pulpit

St. Lukestide, which notes the connection between Church and Medicine, was marked by the appearance of Dr. Maxwell Jones in Loders pulpit. He held the attention of a large congregation with a thoughtful sermon on the Christian attitude to suffering.

November 1950

Target for 1951

In wishing our readers a happy and a prosperous new year, we follow the example of the Press, and season the wishes with good advice. The parish might well take as its motto for 1951 the opening verse of one of the Psalms, 'Behold, how good and joyful a thing it is, brethren, to dwell together in unity.' Nothing is more effective in spoiling the life of a small community like ours than an undercurrent of bad feeling between neighbours. If we in the parish of Loders, with all our great blessings, cannot be one happy family, how can we expect the nations of the world to be one? It is no use wishing

for the time when war shall be no more unless we get to work
and eradicate from our hearts our warlike disposition towards
neighbours whom we happen not to like. World peace cannot
be got for us by any conference of statesmen. It has to begin
in our own hearts and in our own parish.

January 1951

'Silent night, holy night'

The midnight communion on Christmas Day is still growing in
popularity. The congregation which filled the nave was the
biggest ever. Worshippers had the pleasure of a walk in frost
and moonlight. Those who got to church early had an unusual
experience of the church. There was no other light save that of
the two candles on the altar, the coloured lamps on the tree,
the lamp in the crib, and a soft moonlight suffusing the
windows. It was indeed, 'Silent Night, Holy Night'.

January 1951

Parties in Lent?

The outward marks of Lent in Loders will be a weekly service
at three on Thursday afternoons (the first Thursday excepted);
some sermons from the Vicar of Powerstock on Sunday mornings, and a sermon by the Rector of Bridport on Good Friday
morning. The inward marks, visible to God alone, should be a
deepening sorrow for sin, and a growing desire to be made like
unto Jesus Christ, who is what human nature can, and must,
be. We may go to parties in Lent, and still be keeping Lent,
provided we have these inward marks.

February 1951

Furrows to heaven

The Farm Service will be held in Loders Church on Trinity
Sunday, May 20th, at 7 p.m. Farmers and their men, especially those living at a distance, have found it rather a rush to
get to church at 6.30., so this year it will be half an hour later.
By right the service should have been on Rogation Sunday, but
the wetness of the season had held up ploughing, and it would

have been unrealistic to pray for a blessing on supposedly growing crops which had not been sown. Last month, the continuous rain made it appear that the ground could not be ploughed in time for spring sowing, but a fortnight of drying weather, combined with dawn to dusk ploughing, has saved the situation. A shoulder of Boarsbarrow has just been ploughed, and from the valley beneath it looks as if the long straight furrows are running right into heaven.

April 1951

Godly tonic

By a lucky coincidence, Fête Day is also the eve of Loders' patron saint, Mary Magdalene. Coming so close on the Dedication Festival, the Fête will carry on the tradition of Loders Feast. We hope that parishioners will not be so tired by their merrymaking on the Saturday that they will give the go-by to church on the Sunday, for that is the day on which we thank God for having given us such a lovely old church. Sometimes it seems that strangers value our church more than those who were baptised and married in it and live within yards of it. A letter has lately come from Ealing asking the times of services, and another from Bournemouth. The Bournemouth letter says that the restfulness of a Loders evensong is better than any doctor's tonic. We cannot be healthy without God. He is the tonic that moderns need, but they are not aware of this.

July 1951

Question and answer

This is the time of year when Parson's progress through village street and country lane is watched more narrowly than usual. The bolder spirits stop him, and ask, 'When is harvest festival?' Loders Parson was lately far from home. He had strayed into the wildest parts of neighbouring Powerstock. By the wayside he met one of the natives sharpening a billhook with terrible efficiency, and looking decidedly resentful of foreign intrusion. He with the billhook demanded, in ominous voice, 'When be your harvest festival?' 'Second Sunday in October,' said Parson. 'Good,' said he with the billhook, looking less lethal. 'Now we can come to our'n and your'n.' A bit further on, Parson met another of the Powerstock natives, mending a dry wall. This one looked none too friendly either, and there was a heap of stones at his elbow. The wall mender fixed Parson with an aggressive eye and said, 'I would very much like to know when your harvest be to Loders.' 'Second Sunday in October,' said Parson. 'That be very wise,' said the wallmender, letting Parson pass. Rumour has it that the United Christian Council of Bridport has pronounced the old custom of attending as many harvest festivals as you can, to be harmful to the soul, and has decreed that all the local harvest festivals shall be on the same day. Like most rumours, this one is probably untrue, but it is sufficient to imperil the lives of harmless country parsons. In an age when the liberty of the individual is becoming more and more restricted, the countryman will not readily part with his harvest perambulation from one festival to another. And is it so very unchristian to have an urge to sing the harvest with the foreigners in the next village?

October 1951

A revised opinion

Until they attended the recent missionary exhibition in Bradpole, some of our people were dubious about the merits of overseas missions. And not without reason. Once upon a time they were beguiled to a missionary film at Bradpole on the promise that it would equal the best that the cinema could show. The film turned out to be old and worn, its flickerings made the viewers giddy, and the sound track was a man in a box with a bad cold. But the films shewn at this exhibition were excellent. They had been made for the missionary societies by the film trade. They were good entertainment, and they left the viewers uncomfortably aware of the problems confronting Christianity and the necessity of facing them.

February 1952

Armfuls of flowers

The Mothering Sunday rites, now a tradition with Loders Sunday School, were rather damped this year by the rain, but they were carried out more keenly than ever. In spite of the rain, there was a full attendance of children and mothers at church. Flowers were so plentiful that some children brought armfuls. Some also brought presents for their mothers. After service the children went through the village delivering the flowers at the homes of the sick and the aged. Will those recipients who were shaken by the suggestion that they came within either categories please be comforted? There were so many flowers that they were bestowed on most houses, and the children did not stop too long to think.

April 1952

A little logic needed here

Remembrance Sunday is one of the most solemn days of the year. Muffled peals are rung, dead marches played, and people flock to church to honour the lives laid down in the world wars. Yet Good Friday, the day when Jesus laid down his life for us all, has become a holiday. Those who are not out to enjoy themselves, or at least to put in the early potatoes, are regarded as being somewhat odd. Surely a little straight thinking is needed here. From one angle Good Friday is a joyous day, because on it Jesus achieved our salvation. But the cost was so great that nobody with a sense of decency can do other than stand in spirit at the foot of the cross and say, 'This was my fault.'

April 1952

Logic needed here too

Harvest means more to us than any other festival. Something in the golden cornfield stirs the imagination. We enthuse over Harvest because we appreciate the yearly miracle that gives us food and clothing. But our bodies, which Harvest feeds, do not last for long. Clear thinking would make Easter the first of the festivals, because Our Lord's Resurrection opens up the vista of eternal life. Those who are stirred by the cornfield, and not by the spring flowers rising again out of the dead earth, think too much of their stomachs.

April 1952

The book of rules

The Anglican Church imposes few rules on its members, but one of them is that those who are confirmed shall make their Communion at Easter. Please look at the list below for the times of services.

April 1952

Easter 1952 – the Vicar's work-load

Services for April
Loders Maundy Thursday, H.C. 10 a.m.
Good Friday, Mattins 11 a.m.
Easter Day, H.C. 7, 8 and 11.45, Matins 11, Children 2, Evensong 6.
12th H.C. 8, Matins 11, Children 2.
19th, H.C. 8 & 11.45, Matins 11, Children 2, Evensong 6.
26th H.C. 8, Matins 11, Children 2.
Dottery Good Friday, Evensong 7 p.m. Easter Day, H.C. 9, Evensong 3.
12th, & 19th. Evensong 3, 26th. Evensong 6.
Askerswell Good Friday, Matins 10 a.m. Easter Day H.C. 10, Evensong 7.
12th Evensong 6.30. 19th. Children 10, Evensong 7.
26th H.C. 9.30, Evensong 7.

April 1952

'We will remember them'

Good resolutions tend to weaken with the passage of time. The resolve made, when war was fresh in our minds, to keep annual commemoration of those who gave their all, is one we must not get slack about. We till our fields in peace, and the English way of life continues in our age-old villages only because there were Englishmen ready to die to preserve this right. Sunday, November 9th, is their day – Remembrance Sunday. The best way to honour their memory is not in the cosiest arm chair, with the wireless on, and the feet up, and the old pipe puffing contentedly. It is no easy thing that Remembrance Sunday brings back to us. The best way to honour the dead is to come to God's house, where their names

are engraved on the wall, and to kneel wonderingly and prayer-
fully to that spirit of sacrifice which makes human nature
divine. In Loders the main service will begin at five minutes
to eleven, so that in spirit we can keep the Silence with the
Queen at the Cenotaph.

November 1952

Ecumenicalism rings out

Askerswell Bell Fund has received through Mr. Marsh of
Hembury House a donation from Mr. and Mrs. P.W. Day of
Gloucester, who wrote, 'Tell your Rector it's from two
Methodists, with every good wish for success in raising enough
to peal the bells again.' The practical good wishes of these two
Methodists are deeply appreciated. The Noncomformists of
Exeter shew the same spirit, for they have lately given Exeter
Cathedral a pulpit to replace the one destroyed in the blitz.
Inter-denominational acts of kindness like this are reminders
that the differences between Christian sects are as nothing to
the spirit and the truth they have in common.

November 1952

Confirmation sermon

The Bishop of Salisbury, Dr. Anderson, wrote to say how
heartened he had been by the service in which he confirmed
43 candidates from Loders, Dottery and Askerswell. On this
occasion the interior of Loders Church looked like a Hogarth
engraving – only the faces were pleasanter than Hogarth's. The
Bishop stood in the body of the church, talking first to the
candidates, then to the parents, and he had scarcely room to
move for congregation, which crowded the aisles before him
and the chancel behind him. At the west end several young
men found perches on the organ blower, and others on the
window sills. The Bishop's text was a noble one from St. John,
'As many as received Him, to them gave He power to become
the sons of God.' He told the candidates to mark it in their
bibles. Have they done so? They certainly made a good start
with their Communions. At Dottery all the candidates, some
with their parents, attended the Communion on the Sunday

after the Confirmation, so that the congregation was bigger
than on Easter morning. All the Askerswell candidates made
their Communion, too, and so did the majority of Loders. The
candidates at Askerswell wish to thank Miss Edwards for
having the classes in her home and for giving tea to those who
came direct from work. Dottery candidates likewise are grateful to Mr. and Mrs. C. Marsh for having them at their house
and providing such excellent fires. Mr. Marsh, Mr. Robert
Barnes, Mr. Barker and Mrs. Aylmer kindly conveyed candidates to church on Confirmation day. The vicar would like to
disclaim credit for the fancy names that the *Bridport News*
attached to some of the candidates. He is not always responsible for the spelling and punctuation in his own *Notes*.

December 1952

Useful gifts

Loders Church seems never to have possessed churchwardens'
wands of office. When these were needed for high occasions,
the practice was to borrow from another church. Borrowing
will now be unnecessary, thanks to Mrs. Lenthall who has
presented a pair in memory of her late husband. By a strange
irony, we have gained the wands and lost the churchwardens.
When new ones have been appointed, the wands will be fixed
to their pews. The Mothers' Union have presented a blue
curtain for the chancel door in Loders Church. It is for winter
use, to reduce draughts, and Messrs. Wippell have made it a
good match with the altar hangings. Many thanks to the M.U.

January 1953

An example

A Pymore lady who worships regularly at Dottery was ill, and
could not attend church for two Sundays. But she sent her
collection by a neighbour each Sunday, with the very true
remark that, 'Bills have to be paid all the same, whether we
are there or not.' Were her example to be generally followed,
the financial part of running a church would not be the continual headache that it is. Worshippers who are wary of trusting
large amounts to their neighbours might discharge their duty

by the simple expedient of doubling their collection after a Sunday's absence.

February 1953

The right balance

Ash Wednesday ushers in the season of Lent on February 18th. Lent was once forty days of unrelieved gloom. Our forefathers used to take a last frolic on Shrove Tuesday in the spirit of a condemned man feasting on the eve of execution. We have gone to the other extreme. If anybody were to object to the date of a dance or a dinner that it was in Lent, the rest of the meeting would turn round and look at the objector with the dropped jaws of blank amazement. As always, the right course is between the extremes. Nothing could have lasted for as many centuries as Lent without good reason. And the reason is, to be found in the name. Lent is simply the old word for Spring. It is the spring of the human spirit, striving like the snowdrops and the primroses to come alive to God. It is a time both of pain and of joy – of pain when it makes us realise that we have been living the life of the flesh and not of the spirit; of joy when it brings us closer to God, 'in whose presence is the fulness of joy and at whose right hand is pleasure for evermore'. For a variety of reasons our three churches cannot make the choice of services wider by offering weekday services in Lent. But the normal Sunday services offer plenty of scope, and may we suggest that attendance at church every Sunday would be a good Lenten resolution? On Ash Wednesday there will be service at Loders at 10 a.m., at Askerswell 11 a.m. and at Dottery 7 p.m.

February 1953

Easter Vestries

Easter Week is the traditional time for a parish to receive the balance sheet of church accounts, and appoint churchwardens, sidesmen and church council. Every parishioner is eligible to come, and ought to come. We owe it to those who do our jobs to shew an interest.

February 1953

Easter in Church

Another Easter is passing into oblivion. Ecclesiastically, as
distinct from those who suffered by the weather, it is a pleasant memory. Each of our three churches looked beautiful in its
own proper style. Plenty of garden flowers were available to
the decorators, and these were supplemented by the thousands
of primroses, and wild daffodils, gathered by the children on
Good Friday. Colour schemes were predominantly yellow. At
Askerswell the cross worked on the white altar frontal by Miss
Edwards evoked much praise. Loders music was up to its usual
high standard, and the congregation that sat and listened to
Stainer's anthem 'Blessed be the God and Father', were appreciative. Askerswell choir, shewing signs of the expert tuition
given it weekly by Miss Wilkinson, sang another beautiful
anthem of Stainer's, 'They have taken away my Lord'. The
total number of communicants was about the same as last year,
Loders 90, Dottery 30, and Askerswell 35. In proportion to
size, Dottery's was easily the best achievement. The total
attendances at church on Easter Day were about 450, which is
not bad for a combined population of 750. The contribution to
the Vicar's stipend, commonly called the Easter Offering, was
the highest on record, £30.4. (Loders £27. 12s. Dottery £2.
12s). Askerswell does not figure in this because it has to pay
a levy of £12 towards the Clergy Incomes Assessment.

May 1953

St. Mary Magdalene's Day

The Dedication Festival of Loders Church is on St. Mary
Magdalene's Day, the 22nd July, but it will be kept up on the
following Sunday. The main object of the festival is to thank
God for having given us such an old and lovely church as
Loders. If ever you pass some of the churches which our
generation has provided, you will grasp the extent of our
indebtedness.

July 1953

Ecumenicalism in practice

The Wesleyan Chapel in Uploders has been re-opened for a fortnightly service. The new Methodist minister in Bridport, and the lay preacher in Bradpole who is his chief assistant in the enterprise, are advocates of anything but a defeatist policy, and feel that a shut-up place of worship is a reproach. They are bolder spirits than the previous Minister, who took no further step after circularising Uploders with a letter saying that the re-opening of the chapel was contemplated, and asking whether support would be sufficient to meet expenses of maintenance. Our own sympathies lie with the bolder spirits. We wish them good luck in the name of the Lord, and hope that they may be able to rekindle the spirit of public worship in Uploders. They are well placed to do this.

July 1953

CHAPTER 4

Of campanology, male chauvinism and bibulousness

An unholy trinity

After the sober titles of the first three chapters, this title may seem wordy, and the items peculiar bedfellows. But the Vicar was an avid and skilful bellringer. He could 'set' the one-ton Loders tenor bell in its upside down position with gentle precision. He had a firm grasp of complicated mathematical bell-ringing series learnt in youth. In this and other matters he had a phenomenal memory, particularly of the literary extracts learnt at Kelham. He would test the patience of his nearest and dearest by re-telling long tales learnt many moons ago. He knew much of Chaucer's Prologue to the *Canterbury Tales* off by heart, and he could recite the first chapter of the *Gospel according to St. John* in Greek, and from the Authorized Version (which was 'the only version'). At

Kelham he had become accustomed to the monastic day, with gardening and wooding interspersing study and prayer.

He was proud to consider himself a Victorian father. He eschewed washing up, and left all housework to 'the varlets' – usually his children. Having been in a monastery and in the Officers' Mess of the Honorary Artillery Company, he thought he knew a woman's place. To counteract this prejudice, he often indulged ladies in unctuous hyperbole. He didn't approve of homosexuals. He showed early fears that the collapse of the British Monarchy might be caused by fragile marriages, rather than anything political. He supported wholeheartedly the work of the Mothers' Union and the Women's Institute, with his tongue fixed firmly in his cheek.

This cast of mind might have been difficult to accommodate, if his interest in the pleasures of alcohol had not leavened his prejudices with the yeast of a generous kind of banter. At Frome Grammar School he formed an after-school club called The Laughter Club. His humour made his other *faux pas* (for example, see page 81, July 1948) almost forgiveable. The Vicar loved his drink, nowhere near as much as his Bible, but then, they were different. He very much approved of the story of the wedding in Cana. He very much approved of weddings in general – if they lasted – and of wedding receptions in particular. At these events he was often a focal point, making a speech, sometimes impromptu, but always with witty vigour. He would laugh in an infectiously thunderous manner, whilst holding his glass firmly in hand.

At the Vicarage, he brewed his own beer for several years, placing the jars in the airing cupboard under all the drying clothes ('woman's work'). His brew caused strange odours and froth to percolate the linen. For a time he became an expert in making mead from Forde Abbey honey, as if his Vicarage were a complete Benedictine monastery. He regarded publicans of the parish as the pivot of society. They were necessary attendants on Ringers' Outings, as the 'physicians' of the Ringers (particularly of Harry Crabbe, captain, or vice-captain, depending on the year). Ringers' Outings were known in Dorset language as 'Out-Ins', for obvious reasons. The Vicar was a connoisseur of Bridport India Pale Ale on Draught brewed by J.C. and R. H. Palmer. He had less time for their Ordinary Bitter, which he dismissed as 'Boy's Beer'. He filled the compact Vicarage cellar with strong red wines from Burgundy – bottles of Châteauneuf-du-Pape showing his catholic tastes – which later graced the long dining-table in a muscular way. He often sang from the psalms about 'wine that maketh glad the heart of man'. He always had 'a little something' to please the taste of all guests, and sometimes he was barman for prodigious numbers, as when the Choir returned from carol-singing and needed thirsts quenching. He had a good head in the bibulous sense of the word, and most others, but he did have a sneaking admiration for his Captain of Ringers, who had a legendary power of retention. On the way home from Dartmoor, when he was mounting the coach after a timely stop at a 'port of call', he begged Harry Crabbe to bequeath him his bladder, if the latter were to predecease him. Read on!

Ladies need not apply

The Ringers have a few vacancies for their charabanc outing to Portsmouth on Saturday, July 17th. Ladies need not apply. Most of the ringers are married men, with decided views on what constitutes pleasure!

July 1948

Men wanted

Choir practice will begin again, after the summer break, on Aug. 20th. The choir badly needs more men, especially for the harvest anthem.

August 1948

Gay ladies

Will this have been a record year for parish outings? The Mothers' Union have been to Wells, the choir to Bournemouth, the Ringers to Portsmouth, the Women's Institute to Torquay, and the Children's Outing is yet to come. All except the Ringers were lucky in the weather, the Women's Institute notably so, for while the B.B.C. were scaring us with gale warnings, they were basking in Mediterranean sun at Torquay. Yet nobody had a jollier day than the Ringers. They can stand any amount of external moisture as long as they are not dry within. The nine Loders Ringers were accompanied by their chaplain, their brewer, and twenty all-male supporters. On the way to Portsmouth they stopped, and the Ringers pulled the bells of Bere Regis Church. When they came out of the tower, a glance at the stocks of refreshment showed at once that the twenty all-male supporters were alarmingly expert at pulling of another kind. But all's well that ends well. The morning after was a Sunday, and the Ringers were manning Loders bells dead on time – just as if nothing had happened.

August 1948

Happy month!

A parson's life has been described as 'A succession of disappointments bravely born'. November brought the Vicar so much encouragement, and so little to scold the parish about that he wonders whether he really is a parson. All Saints Day was a Monday, and rain was emptying itself down. The Vicar feared he might be celebrating the All Hallows Communion on his own. But by ten o'clock he had a crowd of mothers, including a dauntless band from distant Dottery. They were working mothers, too, for whom Monday is Monday.

December 1948

Doubles for Prince Charles

A quarter peal of Grandsire Doubles, lasting about 45 minutes, was rung on Loders bells in honour of the birth of the Prince.

December 1948

An apology – Dottery's princely peal

An apology is due to Dottery. Last month's *Notes* recorded the peal rung on Loders bells in honour of Prince Charles of Edinburgh, but did not mention the peal of loyal Dottery. This was rung, on the solitary bell, by Roger Chubb, aged three.

January 1949

Muffled bells

The Vicar and the People's Warden, Mr Eli Lenthall, represented Loders at the funeral of the Bishop [Dr. Lunt] in Salisbury Cathedral. The vast congregation included six bishops and some 300 diocesan clergy. Loders Ringers rang half-muffled peals.

January 1949

St. John Ambulance in the tower

Congratulations to Mr. Clem Poole, who has won the gold medal of the St. John's ambulance for fifteen years' exemplary service. The wives and mothers of our ringers can take comfort from his regular attendance at the tower, where the consequences of a little carelessness may range from a skinned hand to a broken neck.

April 1949

Curious meats

In one church tower of the Vicar's acquaintance is a ringer who cooks and eats snails by the peck; in another tower is a ringer who eats hedgehog, previously baked in clay. The Vicar was not altogether surprised to learn that a Loders ringer feeds on badger, and waxes lyrical over badger hams.

April 1949

New ringers

On Monday nights in winter the male population of Loders seemed to concentrate in the church tower. Sometimes there was scarcely room to move. In consequence we now have several promising new ringers – Messrs. C. Chard, R. Drake, F. Legg, and C. Legg. It is specially gratifying to have four junior ringers who are keen – Bernard Harris, John Drake, Alan Goldie and Michael Goldie. Three of these live nearer Shipton Gorge than Loders Church, but nothing short of a blizzard keeps them from practice.

June 1949

Ringers and belles

Mr. G. Hyde, of Willow Cottage, Uploders, has a few vacancies for the Ringers' Outing on Saturday, July 9th. The programme is: by coach to Dartmouth, by steamer up the River Dart to Totnes, high tea at Totnes, by coach back to Loders. The price of all this is about 18/- per head. Ladies will be interested to know that this year the ringers do not object to female company, not even that of their wives. So far, there has been no rush of Ladies to fill the coach. Ladies are still allergic to mice, and maybe they are allergic to ringers because these eat badgers, snails and hedgehogs.

July 1949

Not easily explained

As our Ringers were sitting on the deck of the river steamer going up the Dart to Totnes, a photographer was taking snaps of the good-looking passengers and undertaking to send them, when developed, to their addresses. Some days later, one of the Ringers received from this source a photograph of two ladies instead of himself. At the time of going to press he was still in process of convincing his wife that it was a mistake.

August 1949

A gaggle of Ringers

Before the Women's Institute support any more national resolutions to secure better hygiene in the handling of food, they had better take a peep into Mr. Billy Bagg's barn, where a gaggle of Ringers are making cider. What goes into that cider must, however, be concealed at all costs from Miss Butterworth, our apostle of hygiene. She would lose her sleep for ever, and the village would lose a devoted servant.

November 1949

A kindly bishop

We doubt that Loders people know what a good friend they have in Maiden Newton in the person of Mr. John Bishop. For the second time in three years he has overhauled the machinery of our bells. If this very necessary job were done by the bellfounders, we should incur a substantial bill. Mr. Bishop will not allow payment to be mentioned, let alone made. At the end of his Saturday afternoon of hanging upside down among the bells with a spanner and a grease gun, we give him tea and he thinks we are very kind. Maiden Newton Church is lucky to have him among its parishioners. He has saved them many pounds over many years. We admire his readiness to do anything for the House of God, anywhere.

December 1949

Wedding bells

Flowers, music, bells, and a large congregation, combined to make a notable event of the wedding of Miss Ann Crabb and Mr. John Haines. The flowers were given by the Women's Institute, of which Miss Crabb was a member, and were displayed with all the skill at the command of Mrs. David Crabb and Mrs. Harry Legg. Mr. Tiltman played wedding music, and the bells were not slow in saluting a bride whose father and brothers are ringers. It was surprising to discover that most of the large congregation, comprising nearly a quarter of the village, were relations of the bride. Miss Crabb broke with the powerful local tendency in marrying, by going to London for a husband, and that alone should win her the blessing of eugenists. We wish her, and her husband, every happiness, but it is hard to forgive him for taking away a regular member of the Sunday evening congregation.

March 1950

Mind over matter

A party of working men descended on the Travellers' Rest. They drank their beer with no sign of relish. Indeed, the signs were all the other way. 'Watery stuff, this,' they said. 'Can't we have some of the new Bridport beer?' The Landlord replied in the affirmative, and refilled their pots. This time there were grunts of approval all round, and such remarks as, 'Now this is what you can call beer.' The Landlord smiled. Both samples of beer had come from the same barrel.

June 1950

Spirits undampened

The Ringers will fight shy of St. Swithin when they choose the date of their next outing. He gave them lashings of rain for their trip to Minehead & Ilfracombe, with very few fine intervals, but they and their friends, who filled a 26-seater coach, had an enjoyable day. They managed to get in some ringing at Ilfracombe Parish Church. Sandwiches for the whole party had been provided by the Captain & Mrs. Harry Legg. The Vice-

Captain, Mr. H. Crabb, supplied each ringer with liquid refreshment. Thanks were accorded the Secretary, Mr. G. Hyde, for his excellent arrangements.

August 1950

Cheerful givers

If it is true that the Lord loveth a cheerful giver, he loves Loders. The begging and the giving have of late been prodigious. The ladies of the congregation have fleeced the village on a scale that has made their menfolk blush for shame, and the joke is that one of the ladies got home from a round of fleecing to find that her husband, during her absence, had given much of her cooking fat and dried fruit to another lady collector. The one thing that the Loders male will not part with is sugar.

September 1950

A drink of oil

Dottery bell was out of action for two weeks, and Mrs. Wensley, who rings it, suffered from a sense of frustration which almost moved her to summon together the faithful by whistle or drum. Thanks to Mr. Cecil Marsh, the bell is now fitted with a wire rope. The marked absence of groans as the bell rings, suggests that he also gave it a drink of oil.

February 1951

Prodigious appetites

There is speculation as to how much a Litton Cheney man normally eats. When visiting ringers held a meeting in that village, the Litton Ringers' wives provided a free tea. They had been told to expect fifteen ringers. But to their dismay and alarm, no less than forty-three sat down to the tea they had laid for fifteen. The forty-three found, however, that they could entirely satisfy their hunger, and leave much over of the tea that the Litton wives thought adequate for fifteen. In consequence, some Loders wives are feeling thankful that they don't have to forage for a Litton man.

March 1951

Fraternal Ringers

Powerstock Ringers joined Loders in a recent Saturday after-noon tour. They rang at Toller, Rampisham, Evershot, and Maiden Newton, and came back to their Sunday ringing heavily fortified by the fish and chip supper for which Maiden Newton is becoming famous. Maiden Newton rang at Loders a few days later.

April 1951

Roadside booths

Loders Ringers find that when they take an outing in the direction of Portsmouth, they have no difficulty in filling a bus. Indeed, the Secretary, Mr. George Hyde, had to charter a larger bus at short notice. The weather was perfect, and on arrival at Portsmouth the trippers amused themselves to their several tastes. Some went to the Isle of Wight on to Hayling Island, others went over Nelson's *Victory* at the Dockyard, and others visited friends. The fact that the trippers all chose to bring home either sweet peas or strawberries is accounted for by the stop the coach made at a roadside booth.

August 1951

Grand Old Man of Loders

May we tender our congratulations to Captain Welstead, whose birthday is on Guy Fawkes' Day? Being a man, he will not sue us for disclosing that it is his eightieth. We think he is the oldest member of Loders congregation (but there is always the chance that a lady member may be saying, 'And you can go on thinking that'). Certainly he is one of the most regular attenders. On the rare occasions when his seat is empty there is a good reason. Our wish that there could be more like him will be echoed for the further reason that he is the most popular man in the parish.

December 1951

Remembrance Day

At Loders the morning service was impressive. Commander Streatfield's address touched exactly the right note, and the Dead March from 'Saul', as performed by the organist, made a fitting finale. A word of congratulation to the ringer who rang eleven o'clock on the tenor bell! To do this successfully he had to set the tenor at back stroke. Those who know the reluctance of tenors to be set at back stroke were prepared to hear it strike twelve, or even thirteen, which it did not.

December 1951

Wifely aide

Another bit of good spirit has been shewn by Mr. Bill Tiltman. On a recent Saturday afternoon he could be seen in the church, at the top of a long ladder, replacing a piece of glass that had blown out of a window of the Lady Chapel. The labourer, who stood on the bottom rung and kept the ladder from slipping, was none other than his lady wife. But to nobility of spirit like her husband's she made no claim. She agreed with him that she was only there to save herself from becoming a widow.

December 1951

Never a miss

The Ringers held their annual meeting shortly before Christmas and elected Messrs. H. Legg captain, H. Crabb vice-captain and G. Hyde secretary. Mr. E. Paul was appointed tower warden. We wonder if any ringer can equal the achievement of Mr. H. Legg. He has been a ringer for many years, and neither he, nor his brother ringers, know when he has missed a ringing. This speaks as much for his good health, and the care with which he arranges his engagements, as for his enthusiasm for ringing.

January 1952

The 'absorbent' part of the population

A change of landlords at a village inn is an important event for the absorbent part of the population, especially when the inn is the only one. The Blue Ball at Dottery has passed from the genial presidency of Mr. Blair to that of Mrs. Beach, whose special claim on the goodwill of Dottery is that her mother, Mrs. Fleet, once lived there. Mrs. Blair is recuperating in a bungalow called The Shack, at West Bay.

February 1952

New lease

The Crown, Uploders, has changed hands again. Bad health compelled Mr. Vaughan to terminate his short tenure, and the new licencees are Mr. & Mrs. William Graves. Coming from Stourpaine, Blandford, they like the country, and hope to get rooted here. Mr. Graves has had a varied career. He served in the R.A.F. for eleven years, including the last war, has been a school-master, and now works for an accountant at Dorchester.

March 1952

New pastures

There is a general feeling of regret that Mr. Elston Paul and his family have ceased to be part of the Loders scene. All his working life had been spent at the Court, apart from war service, and the Court will seem different without him. Besides, amiable and placid dispositions are not so plentiful that his can be easily done without. On his last Sunday of bell-ringing the Captain, Mr. Harry Legg, presented him with a book token from his fellow ringers, and the Sunday School gave Jennifer a Bible, and Christine a book of Bible stories. The family has gone to live near Guildford, which will put Mrs. Paul within easy reach of her old home London.

April 1952

Campanology

An attempt to ring a peal of Grandsire Doubles on Loders bells, to mark the fiftieth birthday of the vice-captain, Mr. Harry Crabb, was not successful. It is almost unnecessary to add that this failure did not damp the celebrations.

May 1952

Physician, heal thyself

Loders Ringers look back with satisfaction on their recent outing to Torquay and Totnes, thence by river steamer to Dartmouth. The weather was perfect, and so were the Secretary's arrangements. Like other V.I.P.s, the Captain never travels without a physician, and this is always the landlord of the Farmers Arms. This year the Vice-Captain brought his physician, too, in the landlord of the Crown. To the suggestion that it might not be in the national interest for two physicians to be on the same outing, the Captain retorted that one of them was a specialist (presumably the landlord of the Farmers Arms, who carried special physic in two little black bottles, from which he dosed nobody but himself). The party returned to Loders with the gratified feeling that their intelligence was one above Torquay, where they had seen chickens on a poulterer's slab, bearing the label 'Dressed', when there wasn't a feather on them.

August 1952

The joys of shopping

Mrs. Clark, the governess of Loders School, relinquishes her post this term. It is two years since she succeeded Miss Wilkes. At a gathering of parents and pupils, presided over by the Vicar, Sir Edward Le Breton paid warm tribute to Mrs. Clark's work, and Mrs. Willmott spoke for the parents. Juliet Willmott presented a bouquet, and Margaret Drake followed with a packet of treasury notes, intended to give Mrs. Clark that pastime beloved of wives and dreaded by husbands – an afternoon's shopping.

August 1952

In their element

The ceilings of Loders Church, damaged by the infiltration of water through the old lead roof, have been made good, and whitened. The plastered parts of the walls have been creamwashed with pleasing effect, and plaster has been removed from the built-in north door, and from the Easter Sepulchre, to show the stonework. The mess made by the

builders offered scope to the feminine talent for springclean-
ing, and our Mothers' Union, assisted by non-Union
volunteers, gave two days to scrubbing and polishing, and
made a professional job of it. So infectious was their example
that the two Harries caught it (Harry Legg and Harry Crabb,
captain and vice-captain of the Ringers). These spring-cleaned
the church tower, providing a study in methods. For while the
ladies worked quietly and delicately on the dust of the church,
raising not a speck, the two Harries made bedlam in the belfry
above from whose louvres came clouds of dust, and an occasional jackdaw's nest, no respecters of heads in the churchyard
below. The Harries are sure that they made a better job than
the ladies, which is saying something.

December 1952

Following the Bible precedent

The book of the Acts relates how the Apostles had two excellent candidates for the place vacated by Judas, and settled the
matter by casting lots, the lot falling on Matthias. Loders
Ringers, at their annual meeting, found themselves in a similar
situation. Harry Legg and Harry Crabb polled equal votes for
the captaincy, so they settled it by casting lots, the lot falling
on Harry Crabb. So the officers now are Captain, Harry
Crabb; vice-captain, Harry Legg; Secretary, George Hyde;
tower wardens Harry Crabb and Harry Legg.

January 1953

A good work

The Allington Mothers' Union has been running occasional
'Quiet Days' at which the ladies are forbidden to talk, and
are encouraged to listen and think. In fairness to husbands
who might press their wives to join the M.U. on the strength
of this alone, it must be admitted that when Loders M.U.
were invited to participate, the Enroling Member got no
volunteers.

February 1953

Death by hanging

Loders Ringers did a Saturday ringing tour of the towers at Stratton, Bradford Peverell, Sydling and Cattistock. The weather was bad, and the vice-captain, Mr. Harry Legg, has since been a victim of 'flu, causing him to miss Sunday ringing for the first time in years. Messrs. W. Symes, C. Rogers, C. Graves and B. Wheeler have learnt to ring this winter. Mr. Graves was not deterred by a narrow escape from death by hanging.

March 1953

A world champion – in honour of the Coronation

To the best of our knowledge, world champions in any of the arts are not in the habit of visiting Loders, and therefore the fact that the world's champion bell-ringer [Mr. Ernest Morris] conducted a peal on Loders bells, in honour of the Coronation, qualifies for mention in these *Notes*.

July 1953

CHAPTER 5

The wit and wisdom of the Vicar

'Le style, c'est l'homme'

❧⊙❧

Elsewhere in this book, the Christian commitment and life work of the Vicar are demonstrated. So is his secular influence on the life of his parishes, and way beyond, via the *Parish Notes*. But there is no better way of arriving at the man himself than by a study of his writing style. Such a study is not heavy, scholarly, stuff – it is simply the recognition of his characteristic habits with words. He was a real craftsman. It is amazing how little there is to edit. He had learnt the art of blotting. His handwriting (see pages 202–3) had made him the official scribe for prize book inscriptions at his grammar school. It was his one form of practical art, apart from rhetoric, and bell-ringing. Even so, a few squiggles and obscure references caused his careful typists to make occasional, forgiveable spelling mistakes or errors of punctuation. Like Thomas Hardy before him, his prose is highly individual, even quirky and at times awkward. Old-fashioned rustic or academic obscurities sometimes block the smooth flow. At all times, however, you can hear his voice and see his warm smile, and sense his thunderous wrath, only matched by his effervescent laugh.

His style is always witty. Apart from one or two patches of ordinary reportage – it is difficult to make changes of address sound exciting – his prose is alive. The play of his intelligence is equally at work when writing an obituary as when describing a Harvest Supper. He delighted in the pithy, summary sentence. It clinched the humorous anecdote – usually at some parishioner's mild expense. He had a witty way of begging for money (for the church) which was compelling. He was someone who stuck his neck out, on paper, and in life. He enjoyed the purple passage describing a scene he loved, heading dangerously towards flowery sentimentality on occasion. He used powerful techniques to reprimand his flock for failing in their duties, or for arguing his case and defeating his opposition. Words were his plaything, and the tools of his trade, and he was a past-master in the use of them. He had been self-trained for journalism with the *Somerset Standard*, but his wide literary grounding at Kelham probably contributed most to the blending of his unique voice. He rarely wrote too much, except where his hobby-horse reached obsessive proportions.

Out of the blue comes a remarkable piece of erudition. Usually, it is from the storehouse of his reading at Kelham. Where did he learn that the Romans used lead for their rooves, whilst the Babylonians and Assyrians used bitumen (see page 119)? Only in retirement did he really catch up with the current theological debate. Tending his home farm and his human flock all the while, he did not have much time for deep study, except of *The Daily Telegraph* and the *Church Times*. The following sequence of extracts provides a chance to hear his voice in its varied tones, and delight in his style.

A parish magazine

A parish magazine does useful work: it helps the Vicar to keep
all his parishioners informed of what the Church is doing. In
a small parish like ours, there are not enough people to make
a printed magazine a paying proposition. This is the best that
can be done at present, and if every home in the parish takes
a copy, the loss should not be more than a few pence.

July 1948

Checked jockey

An interesting figure at the Gymkhana was Mr. Robert
Gordon, a guest of Mrs. Lane. In his day he was as famous a
jockey as Gordon Richards, and won more steeplechases in a
year than any other jockey. His highly original taste in dress is
known the country over. At Loders he was not too startling,

but his sombrero and shoes were of the same pattern as his check suit and socks. He was all of a piece, and watched the events on the back of a nag.

September 1948

No tug-o'war

You may hear a complaint that two tug-o'-war teams from neighbouring villages took the trouble to attend the Fête, and were not allowed to compete. The facts are that these two teams were the only entrants, and they were offered reduced prizes of £2 and £1. Rather unreasonably, they held out for a first prize of £4, and a second of £2, which meant that for their 16/- entrance fees they were bound to collect £6 between them. So there was no tug-o'-war.

September 1948

The sacred ministry

Much of the Bishop's Appeal money goes towards the cost (at least £1,000 per head) of training the 1,500 Servicemen who have been accepted for the sacred ministry. Bear in mind the financial sacrifice these men are making! During their three years' training they earn nothing, and when they qualify, theirs will be a wage which is the joke of the other learned professions.

October 1948

The divine weed

A parishioner asks why no tobacco was sent to harvest festival, seeing it was one of the principal crops of the parish this year? Growers may be reserving thanks until they have emerged safely from smoking their 'divine weed'. Smoke a Loders cigar, and you learn unforgettably that the art is not in the growing, but in the curing.

December 1948

A profitable walk

Some people find it easier to think walking than to think sitting. The Vicar is among them. He was walking and thinking in one of our lovely lanes when a horseman drew up and gave him five pound notes towards the cost of the recent repairs to the school roof. The horseman was by no means a stranger. He had done that kind of thing before, to other good causes. Life is sweeter for incidents like that, and God knows how present life needs sweetening.

February 1949

Easter egg

Mr. and Mrs. Linee, of Lower Loders, were delighted by the gift of a baby son, Terence Edward, born on Easter morning as the bells pealed out for matins. Mother and son are doing well.

May 1949

What a commotion!

The son and heir of the vicarage did not choose the most convenient hour for his arrival on April 26th. His father had to go off to give the lunch hour talk to the Bridport Rotary Club, knowing that he was well on the way. His actual arrival coincided with that of six clerks of the Bridport Food Office, who were busy turning the hall into a ration book distributing centre while the doctor was busy upstairs. But, combined with his being a boy, the distractions seemed more fun, and in the evening the bells of Loders – and the excited bell of Dottery – perfectly expressed the joy and gratitude of his parents, and perhaps of the parish.

June 1949

'Bring out your dead'

There was a suggestion of the Great Plague of London about the device of Miss Holmes and Miss Butterworth for collecting jumble for the fête. In this case the tumbril was Mr. Charlie Gale's pantechnicon. As he drove it along, the ladies went before, clanging a dolorous boll, and chanting, 'Bring out your jumble.'

August 1949

A sweet and aristocratic soul

Mrs. Ann Marsh, of The Bungalow, Uploders, was laid to rest on April 7th. She had reached the ripe age of 87. For twelve years she had been bedridden, crippled, and blind. Yet she was one of the most cheerful people in the village, rejoicing in the blessings of a good home, and always showing more interest in the lives of others than in her own. A sweet and aristocratic soul – one who, like her Lord, was made perfect through suffering!

May 1949

Churchwarden for Tussaud's

Mr. G. F. Gillard, our veteran churchwarden, retired from work in April. He had been at Loders Court for 25 years. Were he not very much alive, his wax effigy might be in Madame Tussaud's, to show the barbarous moderns a perfect specimen of that well nigh extinct race, the Victorian butler. The parish were relieved to know that he felt able to carry on as churchwarden in spite of his 75 years, and he proved it by walking from West Bay to Loders Church (for early Communion) in fifty minutes on Easter Day. On Low Sunday he went one better. He walked from West Bay to Loders *and* back on a leg badly swollen by a fall from a step ladder.

May 1949

A share of the feast

Harvest Festival arrangements are as follows: Loders, Sunday September, 25th at 8. 11, 2.15, and 6.30; Dottery, Thursday, September 22nd, at 7.30, and Sunday, September 25th, at 3.30. The produce will again be sent to Guy's Hospital, London, which acknowledged with warmth the hamper we sent last year. Bridport Hospital and Bedford House are usually surfeited with Harvest Festivals, whereas Guys is another Oliver Twist.

September 1949.

Their model

We have a feeling that the choir are trying to model themselves on the small B.B.C. choir which sings the studio services, and is widely acknowledged to be one of the best things the B.B.C. has produced. This is a good choice of an ideal. Our choir will never be large, and if it can maintain its present performance, it will never need to be. Visitors to the church quite often hang back after service to compliment both choir and organist. Loders people themselves are about as musical as a turnip, but even they were impressed by the harvest anthem, in which the solo bass of Mr. Tilley, and the soprano of Miss Vera Legg, were so nicely matched. Mr. Tilley was once a King's chorister of St. George's Chapel, Windsor.

October 1949

Braving the elements

The setting for the first of the Mothers' Union winter meetings was like that of the witches scene in Macbeth. Rain fell in torrents, thunder rolled and lightning flashed, yet fifteen mothers managed to get to church, and not all of them live on the doorstep, certainly not the Dottery contingent. On the following Sunday the weather was almost as bad. At Dottery the rain rattled on the tin roof, and the wind tried to carry it away, and yet there was a congregation, which included that old stalwart, Mr. Studley, whom the weather and his eighty-two years could not keep away.

November 1949

Where your heart is ...

Loders lived up to its name for generosity in December. Refreshments for the social were so freely given that it made a profit of £12; the children's sale produced £17, and the carol singing brought another £10. (It was bad for our souls to read that the Bridport carol-singers only topped £6). Add to this the church collections of £10 on Christmas Day, and it means that Loders contributed some £50 to the work of the Church in December. The regular congregation is glad to have this support from the parish at large. Like all other costs, the cost of maintaining the Parish Church, and of fulfilling the duty of the parish to the Church in general, keeps on rising. It is now beyond the scope of the Sunday collections. We begin the New Year fortified by December's evidence that Loders' hearts are in their church, even the bodies are not.

January 1950

A devout dog

Tessa, the Vicarage dog, came into church while the churching of a mother was in progress, assumed a reverent posture between the mother and the Vicar, and insisted on being churched. We are troubled. We did not know there were puppies, and we cannot find them.

January 1950

A burning question

The answer may now be given to the persistent question: 'When is the next social?' It will be on Shrove Tuesday, Feb. 21st, at 7.30 p.m., at the Hut. We shall thus be 'going continental' in having a last fling before Lent.

February 1950

Sin of omission

The following poem is culled from the Lyme Regis parish magazine. It is equally true of Loders:-

'That Sick Person'

So the Doctor called to see her,
But the Vicar did not go;
For the Doctor had been sent for,
But the Vicar did not know.
Now the Doctor gets his bill paid
With a useful little cheque,
But the Vicar, for not knowing,
Simply gets it in the neck.

March 1950

Easter offering

The contribution made towards the Vicar's stipend on Easter
Day amounted to £23. 0s. 3d. (Loders £20. 11s. 0d.; Dottery
£2. 9s. 3d.) He wishes to extend his thanks to those who were
not at the Easter Vestry to hear them, and especially to those
old people and invalids who sent their offering. The goodwill
behind the offering was even more precious than the offering
itself. Churchpeople everywhere are always saying it is not fair
that the Easter offering should be subject to income tax. In the
last Parliament a group of M.P.s fought hard to get it
exempted, but in vain. The Law Lords took the view that the
Easter offering is a voluntary payment for services rendered,
and not a gift. The Income Tax authorities argue that as the
Church authorities reckon the Easter offering to be part of the
benefice income, why shouldn't they? Let us hope that the
gentlemen at Dorchester are not readers of the Bridport News.
They might argue that the load of stable manure, included in
this year's Easter offering, is worth its weight in gold.

May 1950

Racy news

Miss Butterworth writes from her new home: 'We are nowhere
near straight yet, as we are held up for a carpenter, but we
don't much mind, as we are concentrating on catching the
season in the garden.' How characteristic of her! By a coincidence, the house in which she and Miss Holmes have taken up
residence was inhabited by an ancestor of Miss Holmes in the
early 17th century. By another coincidence, the parish magazine of their new parish is almost exactly like ours. Miss
Butterworth complains that their magazine is not as 'racy' as

ours. We suppose that they lack our Derbys, our Ascots and our Newburys.

May 1950

'Souled' and 'heeled'

Mr. Walter Tudball, our village cobbler, has not been deterred by the weight of his years from going to Weymouth for an operation. His joke is that he is tired of a milk diet, and the operation will reintroduce him to roast meat and vegetables. We await with some anxiety his first encounter with the meat. But be it never so tough, a cobbler can put it to some use ...

Readers who were interested in our report that the village cobbler, Mr. Walter Tudball, had gone to hospital, at the age of 82, for an operation which he hoped would take him off a milk diet and allow him to eat meat and vegetables again, will be pleased to know that he came out of hospital miraculously cured. Callers at his shop saw him sitting beside a fire, the picture of health, boiling the coveted meat and vegetables.

June and July 1950

Angels unawares

'Be not forgetful to entertain strangers; for thereby some have entertained angels unawares.' So says the *Epistle to the Hebrews*. And it is true. The day before he was going into hospital for an operation, the Vicar met two strangers, a lady and a gentleman coming out of the church. The gentleman looked decidedly tripperish. He had been scanning the notice board. 'We hope to come to your Dedication Festival on Sunday,' he said. 'You will be very welcome,' said the Vicar. 'I am afraid I shall not be there. I have to go into hospital, and I cannot for the life of me find anybody to take the services on Sunday.' 'Shall I?' asked the tripper. He turned out to be Canon Buckley, sometime Precentor of Chester Cathedral & Master of the Choristers, now Vicar of Gulval, in Cornwall.

August 1950

A money-box in his car

When the parish church of St. Mary, at Walton, Liverpool, was bombed in 1941, nobody was more upset than Mr. John Sankey, an engineer who had worshipped in this church and loved it. Being a man of action, he put a money box in his car for the St. Mary rebuilding fund, and the many people to whom he gave lifts put donations in the box. He never asked for a donation, but his box yielded £490, which he has just sent to the Rector of Walton.

October 1950

Matriarch celebrates

Another luminary of the world of licensed victuallers, Mrs. Pitcher, celebrated her ninetieth birthday on November 19th. She is the mother of Mrs. Osborne, hostess of the Loders Arms, and of Mr. Tom Pitcher, host of the Farmers Arms. She has been confined to bed for some weeks, but her mind is clear, and her interest in village affairs unwavering.

December 1950

Mrs. Gale's nose

The Mothers' Union visits to the pantomimes at Weymouth and Exeter have not been good for the nose of that good-humoured and tireless church worker of Dottery, Mrs. Gale. In the teashop at Weymouth Mrs. Gale fell on her nose, and precipitated a copious bleeding. In the teashop at Exeter Mrs. Gale fell on the same nose, and nearly broke it. She made light of the exquisite pain, and now she laughs heartily at her misfortunes, assuring sympathetic enquirers that the connection between her nose and Christmas is other than might be imagined.

February 1951

Mrs. Brown's hat

The Mothers' Union trip to Exeter cost Mrs. Brown, of Dottery, a new hat. When she was crossing a bridge, her hat blew into the River Exe. No male passenger was gallant enough to go in after it, and the hat was not insured. The M.U. came back with a poor opinion of the men of Exeter. 'How were they to know,' queries one mother, 'that there wasn't anybody beneath the floating hat?'

February 1951

The concealed button

Colonel Scott's hobby is the working of tapestry, and the re-covering of elegant armchairs. Fine samples of his craftsmanship are to be seen at the Old Mill. He offered to make two collection bags for use in church, and this was readily accepted. It was not until the bags had come to church, and had received their meed of admiration as being the work of a mere man, that the congregation realised how friendly they were with their graceless old collecting plates. A student of church law informed us that legally we were wedded to the plates. We could not put them away without infringing the rubric which directs the collecting of the alms in 'a decent bason'. So we effected a typical English compromise. We use the plates at matins, and the bags at other times. The question is being debated whether plates are less moral than bags. Aesthetically there may be a great difference between them, but ethically there is little. The plate may advertise the ten shilling note, but the bag may conceal the button, and what manner of churchwarden is he who would say, 'Give me the button every time'?

February 1951

Second Vicarage son

Mrs. Willmott and the Vicar wish to thank the parishioners for the many kindnesses shewn them at the recent birth of their second son. Both mother and son are doing well, and we are pleased that it is a son. As an old parishioner puts it, "Michael's sisters will no longer be able to say to him, 'We have a brother, but you haven't'."

February 1951

A kind of junior anthem

Dottery children delighted the congregation on Easter Sunday afternoon by their rendering of a kind of junior anthem. They had been coached by their teachers, Miss Thelma Cleal and Miss Doris Parker.

April 1951

Like Piccadilly Circus

The other evening, the road outside Loders School suddenly became alive with cars. There seemed to be cars everywhere. The Askerswell bus had difficulty in getting through, and the need for a policeman on point duty was too apparent. Every cottage window along the route was manned by every available head, and somebody asked whether this galaxy of cars might not mean that the Food Office had come to give out ration books. But the observant, noting, the sprinkling of knights, baronets, parsons, farmers, doctors, architects, and captains in the crowd, declined to support this theory. As a matter of fact, the crowd and the traffic congestion was nothing more than a meeting of the Church Councillors of Allington, Bradpole, Askerswell and Loders with the Archdeacon of Sherborne and the Bishop's Pastoral Reorganisation Commission. The Commission wanted to know what the parishes concerned thought of a proposal that Bradpole, Loders and Askerswell should be ministered to by one parson (with the help of a lay reader), and that West Loders, commonly called Dottery, should be joined to Allington. The number of councillors who responded to the Archdeacon's summons shewed how lively was the topic. Chairs, even bedroom chairs, had to be borrowed from the cottage of Mrs. Whittle, opposite the school, and the councillors still left standing consoled themselves that at least they were on the right side of the door.

After a long discussion, it became clear that Loders and Bradpole were not very willing to lose the exclusive right to a parson, and Askerswell did not mind throwing in its lot with Loders, provided Chilcombe came with it. (Now Chilcomb is betrothed to Burton Bradstock). If the Commissioners once believed that Dottery did not care to whose star its wagon was hitched, they do so no longer. For Dottery provided the surprise of the evening. Mr. Cecil Marsh, Warden of Dottery, who is not normally given to oratory, made the speech of his life, showing why Dottery should not be severed from Loders, and why he thought the principles on which the Commission was working were wrong. The Archdeacon, had he not been stunned by the force of Mr. Marsh's argument, might have thought it odd that half of the crowded room should consist of Dottery 'Councillors', with feet and tongues and hands loud in support of Mr. Marsh, when the latter, officially, has only one Dottery Councillor to support or disagree with him. The Lay Rector of Loders (Sir E. Le Breton) won the undying gratitude of Dottery by a fighting speech in which he made much of the iniquity of joining a part of a low church parish like Loders with a high church parish like Allington. This speech lost something of its force when the meeting learned that Sir Edward's own Vicar was a near-papist, and the Vicar of Allington was an ex-Baptist. (This on the open confession of the Vicars themselves).

May 1951

No cause for alarm

When the verger, Mr. Thomas, opened Loders Church one morning, he found a seagull, which had evidently spent the night there. Mr. Thomas considered this an omen of high significance, and so did other village sages to whom he confided his discovery. Some thought that it pointed to the death of the Vicar, who it may be guessed, is less allergic to seagulls than he now is to dogs. However, there is no cause for alarm. Our good witch, who helps us at fêtes, says there is no occult significance in the event. Now (says the witch), had it been a magpie, the village might well be shuddering ...

May 1951

Three helpings of rooks

Eighty-four rooks fell to the guns in this year's shoot at Loders Court. A tribute to rooks (kindly dressed for cooking by Miss D. Crabb) was delivered at the Vicarage, and duly converted

into pie. If there be any question as to whether rook pie is
appetising, let it be settled by this, that Master Michael
Willmott, still in the peevish mood that follows measles, and
quite 'off his oats', devoured three helpings.

June 1951

Proud as peacocks

Nothing but praise is heard of the Mothers' Union Festival
held in Loders on Midsummer Day. Mothers of the Bridport
Deanery packed the church right up to the altar rails, and
Loders, and the sun, did their best to make the day memorable. The Ringers took time off from work to give the
mothers a welcoming fanfare on the bells, the organist did likewise to be at the organ, and the President and several members
of the Women's Institute nobly worked in the heat of the Court
kitchen, brewing tea, so that all the members of Loders M.U.
might attend the service. Even the peacock did his bit. He
strutted up and down the churchyard wall in all his glory, and
enchanted the children. Tea, and such a tea as only Loders can
produce, was served on the lawn of the Court. Sir Edward and
Lady Le Breton gave their guests the freedom of the house and
grounds, and they wandered at will. It is regretted that those
who explored the kitchen garden of the Court mistook it for
the Vicarage garden. The Enroling Member of Loders M.U.
(Mrs. Lenthall), and the members are to be congratulated on
their arrangements.

July 1951

A grave case

Loders Churchyard has become an object of public interest, and even of strong feelings, perhaps for the first time in its long history. Any of our readers is apt to be seized in the village street, led into the churchyard, and have pointed out to him the desecrations committed by the Vicar, so the Vicar would like to get in a word of explanation here. When Mr. Elliott took over the cutting of our churchyard last year, he found that it was really more than he could cope with. Often he does not leave work till late, and he was already committed to several spare time jobs. The Vicar helped him last year by cutting the margins of the churchyard with a Rotoscythe (a machine which cuts by a propellor movement). In May this year the Vicar tried cutting the whole churchyard with the Rotoscythe. An abundance of tombstones, curbs and mounds made the manipulation of the machine difficult, but it was done. In this first cutting by Rotoscythe it was noticed that graves which had been kept clipped by relatives were no trouble, and that neglected ones were very troublesome, because a Rotoscythe cannot cut mounds, or inside curbs, or close under tombstones. It was clear that if neglected graves were left, they would spoil the general effect of the cutting, unless the Vicar went over them with the shears afterwards, and this, with his own large garden and lawn, he simply hadn't time to do. He had put an appeal in the magazine of May, 1950, to those having graves to keep them clipped, and he assumed that graves remaining unclipped a year later had nobody interested in them. So he himself lowered the neglected mounds, and was helped by the men of the Church Council to move some of the stones from neglected graves to temporary resting places round the churchyard walls. This made the second cutting by Rotoscythe much easier, and there is hope that God's Acre may cease to be a wilderness, and become what it should be – the best kept garden in the parish.

Some people with flattened graves are reasonable when the matter is explained to them. Others are the opposite. These latter insist that the graves were not neglected, and that they are private property, and no Vicar has a right to touch them. To which the answer is that all the graves that have been lowered have been under observation for a year, and have not been clipped by relatives in that time. The idea that anybody can buy a bit of a parish churchyard and make it private property is an illusion. No Vicar has any power to sell the churchyard, and nobody has an exclusive right to a grave unless it is covered by a faculty from the Salisbury Consistory Court. The Vicar wishes that those who are threatening to see a lawyer would do so.

July 1951

Dorset meets Oxford

The Womens' Institute spent a highly enjoyable day together in Oxford. This year they were favoured with a coach which they didn't have to get out of when they went up steep hills. The doyen of the party, 84-year-old 'Granny' Hyde, says it was the best outing she has had, but she considers that the Oxford housewives aren't a patch on Loders, because 'the outsides o' they old colleges want a turrable lot o' dusting.'

August 1951

The Uploders Charities

Old parochial charities are often a headache to those who are charged with the administration of them. There are two such charities in Uploders, one called the Mellor Charity, disposing of about £2. 10s. per annum, and the other, called the Poor Lot, disposing about £7. 10s. When the present Vicar came to Loders he was told by the administrators that these charities were no concern of his, and for this he was profoundly thankful. Jealousies swarm like wasps round old charities, a few administrators avoid being stung. So the Vicar was glad to be clear of it all, and to leave the charities in the hands of Mr. Gillard and the Parish Council, who satisfied everybody, and seemed wasp proof. But this happy state of affairs was not to last. In 1950 the Charity Commissioners for England, who control all charities, were doing a periodic check, and they required the Vicar to give an account of his administration of the Uploders Charities. Having had nothing to do with the charities, he was unable to comply, and he referred the Commissioners to Mr. Gillard and the Parish Council. The Commissioners objected that these were not the official trustees, whereupon the Vicar asked the Commissioners to clarify the position. This they have done, with the following result: each of the two charities has a separate board of trustees. The trustees of the Mellor Charity are the Vicar and the two Churchwardens; the trustees of the Poor Lot are the Vicar, the two Churchwardens, and two trustees appointed by the Parish Council. (At their last meeting the Parish Council appointed Mr. Charlie Gale and Mr. Herbert Bartlett as their trustees). Having made it clear who are the trustees, the Commissioners stated when the charities are to be distributed, and to whom. Both charities are to be distributed at Christmas time. The Mellor Charity is to be a cash distribution to certain poor persons of Uploders, and/or to poor parents with children at school. The Poor Lot is a fuel charity, to be distributed as coal or firewood to the poorest inhabitants of Uploders. The Commissioners suggest, and few would disagree with them, that the poorest people today are those receiving public assistance and old age pensions. It is a pity that the Uploders Charities are so small. Under the old system the total of £10 was divided last year among 113 persons, who received two shillings or a shilling each! When so small a charity is spread so wide and so thin, nobody really benefits, and the purpose of the charity is defeated. Under the new system a few old persons will each receive a few hundred-weights of fuel at Christmas. The people of Uploders are warm-hearted, and they will readily sacrifice their shillings for the old people. And after all, this fuel is the old people's by law.

September 1951

The supreme sacrifice

Remembrance Sunday falls this year on November 11th. This will please the British Legion, who incline to the idea that the eleventh hour of the eleventh day of the eleventh month, whether it be a Sunday or not, is the proper time to do homage to the dead of the two world wars. Some people hold that a Remembrance on any day is a mistake. They think that it only harrows the feelings of those who lost their dearest and their best. There may be ground for this opinion, but the size of the congregation that attends the Loders Armistice service shews it is not generally held here. On the contrary, relatives of our Loders dead say it is comforting to be caught up in a great national act of sympathy and homage on November 11th. Muffled bells are rung, dead marches played, and poppy wreaths laid, not in glorification of war, but in recognition of the awesome fact that true progress is only got the hard way, through self-sacrifice. Civilisation will indeed be rotting when it cannot see the splendour in men laying down their lives to prevent an evil thing from overtaking their kin and their posterity. Of the dead in the world wars it has been truly said, 'They loved what is decent more than they feared death'.

November 1951

The noble army of grandparents

Congratulations to Mr. & Mrs. Harry Crabb on their entry into the noble army of grandparents. A son has been born to their daughter, Ann, in London. Happily, mother and infant are now making better progress than they did at first.

December 1951

Christmas arrangements

These *Notes* are being written in November, when Christmas lies in the dim and distant future. But by the time our readers have them, there will be nothing dim and distant about Christmas, for the children, at any rate, or for the mothers, on whose plotting and planning the delight of Christmas depends – or for father, who only does the paying. The spirit of Christmas will doubtless be taking possession of every home in the parish, but its presence will be most evident in church, which is the one home common to all parishioners. We hope to have the midnight communion on Christmas Eve, perhaps with carols. At matins on Christmas Day the children will sing round the Christmas tree in the chancel, and will receive from it the packets of sweets which the Mothers' Union puts there. We are sure that this homely touch to the service is something that God likes on His birthday. What we are not so sure about at the moment is where the Christmas tree will come from. Sir Edward's estate has been so drawn on for Christmas trees that there are no more available. Has anybody any suggestions to offer, or, better still, a tree?

December 1951

A warm church at last

On Sunday, December 23rd, the matins congregation found an important-looking document pinned to the door of Loders Church. It was from the Worshipful Cyprian Bourne, Barrister-at-Law, Vicar General of the Diocese of Salisbury and Registrar of the Consistorial Court, proclaiming to all and sundry that the Church Council of Loders intended to put in an electrical heating system, and calling upon any objectors to the scheme to lodge their reasons with the said Worshipful Cyprian Bourne within fourteen days of the publication of the notice. When this notice appeared, the heating system to which it referred had been installed and was already a month old! That is how things work in the venerable Church of England. Neither the Worshipful Cyprian Bourne nor the congregation raised an eyebrow at the apparent discrepancy. Only little minds object to the cart going before the horse. Indeed, the Vicar General's proclamation shewed us the measure of our debt to the Archdeacon of Sherborne, who had had our scheme examined by the Diocesan heating expert, and given us permission to proceed while the ancient machinery of the Consistory Court was yet being cranked up. Without the Archdeacon, the business of putting in the apparatus would be just beginning. And without the generous gift of Lady Le Breton to the heating fund – made fifteen years ago – it would not even be that. It is too soon to pass judgement on the efficiency of the system, but it promises well. Instead of stepping into the atmosphere of a vault, and seeing our breath as we talk, we step into a temperate climate, and feel the warmth from under the pews caressing our feet and legs. Our next business, which is being put in hand at once, is to stop draughts. When the church was cold, we could not be conscious of draughts, but now that it is warm, the slightest current of cold air is noticeable. As to the cost of electric heating? It is too early to say yet, but we are advised that it may add between £30 and £40 a year to our expenses. A few kind parishioners are contemplating a scheme for helping to meet the extra cost. But more of that next time.

January 1952

Loaves and fishes – the Vicar's stipend

The question as to what difference Askerswell will make to the stipend of Loders is being keenly debated. To save bloodshed, we give the answer – £125 gross. But as this increase will automatically raise the amount deducted from the Loders stipend by the pensions, dilapidations and income-tax authorities, and swell the petrol bill, the net increase will be much less than £125. Still, it will be welcome.

February 1952

The backbone of the Choir

Mrs. Fooks, who has long been the backbone, and sometimes the only bone, of Askerswell Choir, is pleased to have acquired some flesh. There are now ten members of the Choir. Mr. Harold Spiller continues at the organ, and Mr. Cecil Legg is choirmaster.

March 1952

Annual dinner speeches

Mr. Tommy Bryan, of Court Farm, Askerswell, was lately married to Miss Jean Roberts in the Presbyterian Church in Hull, and has brought his bride to live at Stancombe. We offer them our congratulations and good wishes. Members of the Agricultural Discussion Club and the Young Farmers are wondering what Mr. Eli Lenthall will now find to make speeches about at their annual dinners. It seemed to worry him beyond measure that Tommy shewed no sign of being matrimonially minded. However, we venture a guess at the theme of Mr. Lenthall's next speech. His churchwardenly eye cannot have failed to notice that Stancombe is half in Askerswell and half in Litton, which, when the master of Stancombe is not at the Askerswell service, gives him the benefit of the supposition that he is worshipping at Litton – and vice-versa.

April 1952

Easter as the parson saw it

Noting that he had ten services to conduct in his three churches on Easter Day, some of our readers remarked that the Vicar would be glad to see the end of it. Well, he was and he was not, for the day was happy as well as strenuous. To see why it was happy the gentle reader must accompany the Vicar on his Easter itinerary. The day began at Loders with a seven o'clock Communion. The morning sun gave promise of a bright warm day. It lighted up the spring flowers that bedecked the church, and made the muster of early worshippers admire the beauty of the place. At 7.30 the bells pealed out, and drew another congregation to the 8 o'clock service. Then followed a hasty journey to Dottery for 9 o'clock Communion. (He who thinks that the lanes are clear at this hour is unacquainted with the habits of milk lorries and strolling cows). What delight it was to burst into another beautifully decorated church, and to find practically the whole communicant strength of the hamlet waiting. There was little time for the usual after-service chat. To the road again, and a six mile ride to Askerswell. Here the stately tower was sending out the sweet chimes of its disabled bells, and in the festive church beneath, the faithful of another hamlet were waiting. So numerous they were that the organist suggested a couple of hymns, and these were sung with vigour. The after-service scene of men and women in gay summer frocks, chatting in the churchyard, was a genuine bit of old England. And so to Loders. Cars parked all along the road to the church implied that the congregation might be large. The church turned out to be packed full. There were many visitors, who are always welcome, and, best of all, there were pew upon pew of familiar village faces. The memorable points about this service were the choir's unaccompanied singing of 'Christ our Passover is sacrificed for us', to the Grand Chant, and the number of worshippers who stayed behind for late Communion. If the reader's patience is not short, space is, so we must go quickly through the remaining services. The children's service at Loders was followed by a well-attended evensong, at Dottery, at which Mrs. Roper's first grandchild was baptised. (This is a boy, Nigel – his parents now live at Weston-super-Mare). Loders had a sizeable congregation for evensong, and so did Askerswell. The new Askerswell Choir gave its first anthem, the descant being sung by the Misses Doreen and Sheila Allport. If the young men of Askerswell would come in and balance the ladies, we might get a first class Choir. Loders also could do with more men.

May 1952

Spiritual pride

Mr. Moss, who took services in the Vicar's absence, writes: 'Loders Church is very beautiful, and it was most cheering to have such a large and responsive congregation.' Mr. Carver, who took the Dottery services, said that he enjoyed them. We mention this to save Askerswell from spiritual pride.

May 1952

Statistics

The number of Easter communicants was 153 (Loders, 93 Dottery, 26 and Askerswell 34). The Easter Offering, which is part of the benefice income, was £34. 11s. 4d. (Loders £23. 17s .4d. Dottery £2. 14s. and Askerswell £7.) Askerswell's Easter offering goes this year towards reducing the church debt. The Vicar takes this opportunity of thanking the congregations for their generosity. The Vicarage hens wish it to be known that they also are grateful for an offering of corn.

May 1952

A stitch in time

The parish may be wondering why the Loders annual church meeting decided to hold a fête on Saturday, Aug. 2nd, when the finances are so healthy. To which the answer is that the running of the church laps up most of the collections, and there is nothing left to keep the church itself in repair. The annual fete is now coming to be relied on to cover the annual deterioration of the church building. Business people always make annual allowance for depreciation, and the Apostle warns Christians against being slothful in business. It is as well to recognise that a church, like any other property, is wearing out. By keeping a church regularly inspected, by renewing a rotting timber here, and a crumbling battlement there, its custodians nip trouble in the bud, and save heavy expense later on. The sums now being asked for to do urgent repairs to churches run into thousands of pounds. Had the church councils concerned been depreciation-minded, they – and the public – might have been spared these appeals.

June 1952

A coming of age

Loders branch of the Mothers' Union reached the age of 21 last month, and celebrated it with a birthday party which is still the talk of the parish ladies. Bradpole M.U. were guests, and they,

with the Loders members, made the Uploders room seem much too small. However, the helpers managed to thread their way between the serried ranks of mothers with jugs of tea, buttered buns and delectable cakes, without mishap. Mrs. Lenthall, the Enroling Member, called on the Vicar to cut the birthday cake. He is 'off' carving at the Vicarage because he can never make the joint go round. Here, the size of the cake gave his talent more scope, and he accepted the commission, though not without a feeling akin to sacrilege as he slew that masterpiece of the confectioner's art. If the ladies were shocked by the manly proportions of the slices, they were careful not to shew it by leaving any uneaten. Mrs. Nantes, speaking for Bradpole, congratulated the Loders branch on their twenty-one years of steady progress, and Mrs. Willmott thanked Mrs. Lenthall and her helpers for the work they had put into the party. Miss Juliet Willmott, who has the local M.U. for a godmother, thanked the members for their present of a writing case.

June 1952

Loders Church roof

The work that has been in progress for the last month has not been mentioned in these *Notes* because the *Notes* travel far and wide, and we did not wish to kindle illicit interest in our lead. The lead is now safely delivered to a foundry near London, and the brow of Constable Edrich is smoother in consequence. It is hoped that the lead will pay for our new roofs of slate and bitumen. Had we succeeded in selling it before the price of lead fell, we might have got a capital sum for roof endowment as well as new roofs. That we did not achieve this object was none of our fault. Architects, builders and licensing authorities are too high-minded to be hurried by considerations of £. s. d. It seems that only parsons think of such things. However, we are extremely lucky to have had two hundred years of wear out of our lead roof, and then to have got a new roof by selling the carcase. Our neighbours in Bothenhampton have reason to envy us. The stone tile roof of their church has re-acted to the sea air, and the parish must raise £2,000 to replace it.

Lead has little intrinsic value. Before the war it fetched only £5 a ton, and was one of the cheapest roofing materials. Rearmament is responsible for the present price. Those who feel that because of its antiquity (it was used by the Romans) lead is the proper roofing material for a church, may find consolation in the fact that bitumen is still older. It was used for the flat roofs of the Babylonians and of the Assyrians before them. It was also the roofing material of Noah's Ark.

July 1952

Having in a builder

The ladies who have so kindly given up time to going round Loders collecting for the fête have more than once been asked whether the Church really needs the money? You may judge for yourselves. When the re-roofing has been done, the plaster of the ceiling has to be made good, and whitened; the leaded lights of the Ladye Chapel windows are perished and must soon be replaced; the tower arch has to be filled in with leaded lights; the stone path in the churchyard must be repaired; and then, as if this were not enough, the organ tuner told us brightly that the organ must soon have £200 spent upon it. A country proverb needs revising – the one that says, 'There are three ways of losing money: gambling is the quickest, wine and women is the pleasantest, but fattening bullocks is the surest.' Having in a builder is now the quickest and the surest.

August 1952

Looking back

The weather for Loders Fête on August Saturday was unfavourable for the first time in five years. It was not bad, but merely capricious. It led the organisers a dance, and then gave them the best profit they had ever made on a fête. The other prophets, those who deal in the weather, were not conspicuously helpful. The B.B.C. told us before the event that it was going to be wet, and it was not. The local prophets, whose oracle may be a sensitive toe or a lumbagious back, told us, after the event, that they had known 'all along' that it was going to be fine. So between them we found ourselves holding a fete in the Hut, where the heat was melting Lady Le Breton's ices, and Mrs. Harry Legg was plying the tightly packed multitude with tea, while outside the sun was shining, and the cool lawns of Loders Court were beckoning. To stave off annoyance we had to keep reminding ourselves that fêtes and flower shows have to be laid out in the morning, and that this cannot be done in heavy rain. We felt sorry for the children's fancy dress and for the flower show, which lacked space above everything and also for the bicycle racing, which had to be abandoned. Much work had been put to all these. But the Women's Institute play and the Square-dancing were better in the Hut, where they delighted a large crowd; and Mr. Wilfred Crabb's field, being on a slope, was ideal for the sheep dog demonstration.

September 1952

Fête donations

Forty flower pots, of many sizes (some very large) and all in good condition are for sale in aid of Loders Church repair fund. Also an excellent pair of lady's shoes, size four. They were given to the Fête, and may be seen at the Vicarage.

September 1952

Believe it or not

A housewife at the beginning of evensong in Askerswell Church remembered that she had come away and left a pan of eggs boiling. She communicated the fact to her husband in writing. He stole out of church, and hurried home – a not inconsiderable distance. What we ask you to believe, because it is true, is that he also hurried back, and was in time for the sermon, and incidentally, the collection.

September 1952

Self-help

Four gentlemen of Loders Church Council, viz., Mr. Tilley, Mr. O. Gale, Mr. Sanders and Mr. G. Hyde, devoted a recent Saturday to preliminary repairs to the church path. These have certainly achieved their limited objective of rendering the path safe for the winter. It is pleasant to walk down the path and think what the work did NOT cost.

October 1952

White elephants

The first assault on the debt which hangs round the neck of Askerswell Church like the old man of the sea will be made on Saturday October 11th in the School at 2.30 p.m. Mrs. Aylmer is directing operations, and her weapon will be the jumble sale, that ancient terror of church debts, and the deadliest form of jumble sale at that – one with tea continually on tap. To make the fate of the old man doubly sure, there will be a white elephant stall as well. Our reporter asked Mrs. Aylmer the difference between jumble and white elephant. With the precision of a born commander she replied: 'Jumble is clothes, and white elephant is all that is not clothes.' A dichotomy which makes either jumble or white elephants of us all.

October 1952

Twins at the font

Loders Sunday School children, who love a christening at their service, have lately been gratified. Following on the adopted son of Mr. and Mrs. Masters, the daughter of Mr. and Mrs. Churchill, and the son of Mr. and Mrs. Collier Marsh (of Charminster), they have sung for the twin children of Mr. and Mrs. Green. On this occasion somebody other than the Sunday School was gratified. There was a baby for each grandmother to hold at the font, and had there been triplets, the empty arms of the great grandfather, Mr. George Crabb, who was standing benignly by, were ready to receive one. Fortunately for the Vicar, the twins entered not into vocal competition during the service, but favoured with a half-amused smile.

November 1952

The etymology of flamingos

A date for your diary is Thursday, November 6th, when, from 7 p.m. till midnight, there will be rich entertainment at the Askers Road House, and an opportunity in buying Christmas presents to help Askerswell Church out of debt. Besides the Christmas presents stall, there will be dancing to the tunes of musicians of whose identity we are in doubt because we are only told that they are The Flamingo Four, but of whose talent we have no doubt whatever. There will also be cabaret by the pupils of Miss Dulcie Gibbs. Another date for the diary is December 12th, when the children of Askerswell school will give a concert for church funds. STOP PRESS – The Oxford Dictionary defines flamingo as 'Large long-legged long-necked heavy-billed scarlet-feathered bird.' The word has affinity with 'flammenwerfer', which means 'Machine spouting liquid fire in war'.

November 1952

Butterfly flitting

Both Loders and Askerswell enter the new year the poorer for the loss by death or removal of many staunch supporters. It is hoped that some of our well-wishers on the fringe of active church life will stop in and fill the gaps. Our new confirmees have made a promising start and are regular at their communions. The world being what it is, the odds against their keeping it up are heavy. We can only hope, and pray. We should all do well to make our own the prayer prayed by Sir Francis Drake on the day he sailed into Cadiz in 1587: 'O Lord God, when thou movest thy servants to attempt any great matter, grant them to know that it is not the beginning, but the continuing of the thing, until it be thoroughly finished, that yieldeth the true glory.' Dogged perseverance is a virtue badly needed in these days of butterfly flitting from one brief interest to another.

January 1953

A welcome bequest

Loders congregation were pleased, but not greatly surprised to learn that their late Warden, Mr. Eli Lenthall, had left the Vicar and churchwardens £100 for the use of Loders Church. It was like him to continue in death the support of an institution very dear to him in life. As repairs to the church have now almost emptied the exchequer, it is likely that the money will be invested against a rainy day. The legacy would then replace a nest-egg which saved the church from falling into debt during the war. Mr. Lenthall's kindly thought is a reminder that in the good old-days a portion for the work of God figured in most wills, automatically.

February 1953

Snowballed

Mr. Edward Barnes is the first of that big family of farmers at Bilshay to get married and leave home – if crossing a few fields and working with Commander Streatfield can be equated with the adventure normally associated with leaving home. Mr. Barnes' bride, Miss Walbridge, comes of another well-known farming family, who knew what they were about when they made Beaminster Church the place of the wedding in lieu of their own little church of Toller Whelme, which could not have held the large congregation. A fall of snow made it possible for the bridal party to be snowballed as well as confettied as they left the church. The snowballs seemed to come from the church roof, and had an element of surprise which confetti lacks.

March 1953

The 'faded aristocracy'

Colonel Scott, Vicar's Warden of Loders, has had the reward of months of house-hunting in acquiring an attractive property in Netherbury, (complete with daily help) which he hopes to move into at the end of this month. Netherbury is one of the haunts of the faded aristocracy, and we would not expect him ever to acknowledge us again did we not know that his heart is still in Loders, and that he made every effort to get a house here. Loders Church owes much to his family's example of regular church-manship, and also to the work they put into the gymkhanas and fêtes. If ever they can tear themselves away from lovely Netherbury, they will find a warm welcome in Loders.

April 1953

Echoes of Moloch

During alterations to the Old Post Office in Loders the workmen uncovered a bricked-up oven. They were somewhat reluctant to obey the owner's order to open it up, alleging that unless the skeleton of a cat was found in the oven, bad luck would pursue everybody concerned. It appears to have been an old superstition that you could not brick up a bread-oven without killing a cat and entombing it in the oven. This super-stition is perhaps a relation of one which has left traces in the Old Testament, where it was good for a house to have a human being built into the foundations, and where it made a city wall impregnable to have a king's son built into it. No skeleton of a cat was found in the Loders oven, so the workmen are worried.

April 1953

Local Cinderella

A shoe has been found at the Hut. The Cinderella whose foot it will fit may have the same on application to Miss Randall at Yondover. A little light on the mystery of how the lady got home without it will be welcomed.

June 1953

CHAPTER 6

The diurnal round

Births – Deaths – Farming – The Seasons – Birds – Flowers – and Bees

❧◈❧

The Vicar was town-bred in Frome, Somerset. After that, periods in a strict, high Anglican monastery and in Officers' Messes in the Army might have lured him towards urban existence. But a deep instinct made him a countryman at heart. Perhaps it was a desire to avoid the madding crowd and to rest in a period of English existence where modernity was at a safe distance. The map (see page 206) hints at the idea that he felt West Dorset was the true centre of England, if not the universe.

He never had a telephone at the Vicarage. If the message were urgent enough, the caller could always find him hewing a tree somewhere, or at his solo matins in the church, or tending his strawberries. He had no intention of catching up with the twentieth century. He built up a home farm, with turkeys and geese and chickens, and Primula the cow. He knew the rhythms of the year as well as his Dorset farmers. He was an expert at broad

beans and he dabbled in asparagus. Fruits he allowed to grow,
like blackcurrants and gooseberries, so long as someone else
picked them. He had a soft spot for the fig tree at the end of the
garden, against the churchyard wall. He cared for his calves, and
was particularly saddened when a heifer strangled herself
through the low bars of the gate as she attempted to have a
meal from the fallen apples off the Tom Putt tree. He did not
fight shy of silage and manure, and he could talk country matters
with the best of them. (In a later extract, not published in this
book, there is a witty piece about a misunderstanding over
signs, where a passer-by might have thought 'A1' meant
'Churchillian standard War Efforts. Well done! First class'. Local
farmers, however, knew the sign referred to Artificial
Insemination.) He carried a gun, shot rabbits and pigeons for
supper, and the occasional pheasant. He had exciting escapades
with badgers, foxes, and deer. Camping out one night to defend
his glebe, he unfortunately missed the predator fox with his
twelve-bore and shot two of his own chickens instead.

Later he mellowed and would never harm one of God's creatures. In a touching description of Loders' lanes (see next page)
he vowed he would never pick a wild flower. He left flower
arrangements to the opposite sex. He was appreciative, particularly of the way simple flowers lined the path to the church,
and gently-handled arrangements enhanced the yellow Dorset
sandstone of Loders church. He also praised the task force of
church decorators at Dottery and Askerswell. They could be
relied upon to make something special of Harvest, Easter and all
the seasonal occasions. Like Thomas Hardy, again, he was a
countryman who only wished to be remembered 'for noticing
such things'. Little missed his eye. 'Diurnal' can sound a little
dirge-like, and miserable. It implies the daily, yearly round. This
selection should soon disperse any sense of monotonous year-
repeat. The Vicar had the rhythm of the year.

From a short piece of writing found on the back of an Inland Revenue form, Payment of Tax, written a few years before his death.

Lovely Loders, set in its verdant valley, with the encircling hills and woods; its stream in the valley by which the village road runs, and many houses stand! This is indeed a place of enchantment.

The lanes in spring are like a wild garden – the primroses, violets, bluebells, wild parsley and red campion, followed by wild roses, honeysuckle and foxgloves, all to be left, we hope, for all to enjoy.

Of caterpillars and cabbages

Boarsbarrow, landmark of Loders, and symbol of Loders Women's Institute, is not its usual self. It has been ploughed right up to the belt of trees on its summit. When parishioners heard the tractor, and saw the green mantle of Boarsbarrow turning brown, they thought the food situation must be desperate indeed. But it was also done to save their cabbages. Boarsbarrow had become infested with caterpillars, and a remedy was to plough them in.

July 1948

Shocking news

To be listening to the nine o'clock news, and to hear it announced that your distinguished brother has been killed in an air crash, must be a great shock. The sympathy of the village goes out to Mr. John Gent, of Uploders, who lately had this painful experience.

August 1948

Harvest Festival

Fickle weather did not prevent the local corn harvest from being gathered, and the potato harvest is under way. Some corn had to be cut by mower, and some had grown out. Yet our farmers say that the yield is good. The Ministry of Agriculture estimates that this year's yield beats the ten-year average, and is well above last year's, which is surprising when one compares the golden days of last summer with the leaden days of this. Farmers are appreciative of their men, who were willing to work any hours to get in the corn. It is fitting that Britain's biggest, oldest, and most vital industry should set other industries an example.

October 1948

Reflections

Both Loders and Dottery seemed to make more of Harvest Festival this year. Flowers, produce, and the decorators' art, were of the best, and the attendance at all the services was over 400. Eggs and grapes were given to the sick of the parish, Loders fruit was gladly accepted by Guy's Hospital in London, and Dottery produce was sold for church funds. Local hospitals were inundated with harvest festivals, and did not need ours. Loders Choir received so much congratulation on their anthem that they are working up another for Remembrance Sunday. The second Harvest service at Dottery was very homely. A father had his small baby in a cot at the back of the church, and a black cat strolled in and sat before the altar. As the behaviour of the cat, and of the baby, was exemplary, there was no need to eject either. They might have been trying to qualify for the bottle of milk which was prominent among the decorations. An observer could not note the approving looks that the more solid members of the congregation bestowed on the little keg of cider and the drinking mug as they went out of church. It is no use asking the Vicar who was the happy recipient of the cider.

November 1948

Slings and arrows

The first wonder of Loders is its church. The second is Mr. H.W. Bishop of Yondover Farm. An ordinary man could not have survived the ills and accidents which have been his lot. Recently, the horse he was riding fell on him, and broke his leg in two places. Previous to that, he had been badly damaged in a car accident, and before that he had been rolled on and broken by another horse. Earlier still, there were major illnesses – influenza, duodenal ulcer, and a pleurisy which put him out of action for a year. Every time, he comes up smiling, with his zest for life and horses unimpaired. His chief anxiety is lest his sons should be too ardent imitators of their father. Edgar is not fully recovered from his bad accident of a year ago, and Frank once lost a thumb to a threshing machine. The latest accident occurred shortly before Edgar's wedding to Miss Valerie Thomas, in Wandsworth, and rather spoilt the social part of it. If anybody can take 'the slings and arrows of outrageous fortune' with a shrug and a grin, it is the Bishops.

November 1948

A problem for decorators

The exceptional sunshine has brought out the daffodils and hyacinths. All through Lent they, and pussy palm, have added to the brightness of the church. When Easter comes, the daffodils and the primroses may be over. The decorators must find something for the church then, and are hoping that the May flowers will oblige. Easter is the greatest of the festivals. The Prayer Book refuses to say how many times a year we should make our Communion, but it does clearly direct that Easter shall be one of them.

April 1949

Harry Crabbe's eyes

The sympathy of the parish is with Mr. Harry Crabb in his recent misfortune. When he was fencing at Upton, a nail pierced his left eye, and so badly damaged it that the eye was removed after the Weymouth Eye Infirmary had done what was possible to save it. The pity is that the left eye was Mr. Crabb's 'good' eye. The right eye, which remains, had been injured in an earlier accident.

January 1950

The passing of George Ellery

No – this picturesque character is anything but dead, but he has passed from the Loders scene, to which for many years he had given the rustic touch. 'Doing' for himself in his tumble-down cottage opposite the Loders Arms was getting beyond him, so he sought and obtained admission to the Infirmary at Stoke. By ancient reckoning he would be in minor orders of the Church, for he was once our Sexton, and so had been his father, and his grandfather. By modern reckoning he should have been the announcer of the wireless feature, 'Those were the days', for to him there were no days like those when ale was a penny a pint, and baccy twopence a screw, and the mother of a family could acquire the inside of a pig for a song. Before giving up his cottage, George chalked on a board, 'A few things for sale', and put it outside his door. As an after-thought, he added, 'By order'. Seekers of bargains found George a shrewd salesman, and came out wondering which had got the better of the deal. Two weeks of Stoke, and George was back in Loders to see if the place was much altered. He supped some tea, and pulled at his pipe, over the stove in the Vicarage kitchen, and was certain he had done right in going to Stoke. They already thought well of him there. Why? – Although he had not touched water ALL over, at the SAME TIME, for four years, the bath attendant had told him he was 'cleaner than most'.

February 1950

Mr. Charles Hine

At a time when we are rather gloomy about the impending departure from the parish of staunch supporters of Loders Church comes the gloom cast by the sudden death of Mr. Charlie Hine, of New Road. The local newspapers may safely be left to describe his colourful career as a coachman in the service of the Duke of Atholl, when he drove King Edward VII; and as coachman, during the Great War, to the War Office, when he drove the leading generals – and Mr. Winston Churchill. We like to recount what we ourselves know of his days of retirement in Loders. Our lanes were nicer for the chance they offered of meeting his ample, jovial figure, with his hounds, and his pockets full of rabbits. The soliciting of a subscription from him was fraught with no fears of a snubbing, for he gave generously to good objects. St. Paul's injunction to take a little wine for the stomach's sake was a text he approved of, and his hospitality was a byword. Whenever he could 'make it', he attended Loders Church, not as much out of pity as out of a desire to support a good old English institution. On the long walk from New Road to the church, the condition of his heart and legs enforced frequent rests, and then he envied the vitality of younger folks who were not responding to the bells. He was essentially an extravert, yet he had in him a streak of melancholy, and was given to strong premonitions. When there was hope of his recovery, he was sure he would never see the daffodils again. He even wrote down a few details about himself for these *Notes*, to save his widow being asked for them. He entered the fuller life on Shrove Tuesday.

March 1950

One of twenty-two

The late Mr. Arthur William Studley, of Dottery, was full of distinction. He was, at 82, the oldest member of Dottery congregation, and was one of the most regular. He was also one of twenty-two children, eleven of whom died in infancy. Dottery still misses him acutely at the Sunday service, but recalls with satisfaction that the very last service he attended was the dedication of the new war memorial. His son's name was on this, and it was a project near to his heart.

April 1950

A sad coincidence

It is rare for two next door neighbours to die within a few
minutes of each other, but that happened recently in Uploders
to Mrs. Pritchard and Mr. Eveleigh. Mrs. Pritchard passed
away in Weymouth hospital, to which she had been removed
from Port Bredy Hospital, and was cremated at Weymouth.
Both she and her husband were comparatively new to
Uploders, but they have won many friends, and her death cast
a gloom on the village. Mr. Eveleigh was a native of Dottery,
and was buried at Bradpole, where he had once been sexton.
Nobody seeing his lithe and cheery figure mowing his lawn
would imagine him to be the great sufferer he actually was.

May 1950

'Patriarch of Loders'

This was the epithet applied to the late Mr. John Crabb, and
not without justification. He had reached the great age of 85,
had come of old Loders stock, and had lived all his life here.
Nobody knew more about Loders than he, and he could
conjure up a clear picture of the village as it was three quarters of a century ago. His widow, Martha, is also remarkable.
At an age not far short of her husband's, she was able to do
most of the nursing of his long illness.

June 1950

Mr. Eli Lenthall

The parish has been profoundly stirred by the serious illness
of its churchwarden, who is also conceded to be the best
farmer in the neighbourhood. A measure of his popularity is
that his wife has been quite inundated by sympathetic
enquiries; on one day there were over forty telephone calls
alone. In the ebb and flow of the illness his endearing good
humour has never left him. He has tried to make jokes without
a voice. At the time of going to print, his doctors will not say
that he is 'out of the wood'. Our prayers for his recovery will
be echoed far outside the parish.

July 1950

If wet?

The succession of pouring wet Saturdays is raising the question of what would happen to our Gymkhana and Fête should Saturday, August 5th, be wet. A relentless downpour would extinguish the Gymkhana, but an attempt would be made to carry on the Fête in the outbuildings of Loders Court, and there would still be the Dance in the Hut at 8.30 p.m. The stallholders would certainly want to sell their cakes and other perishable commodities. However, this is not the right note to harp on. It sounds as if we lacked faith in King Sol, who did us fine in '48 and '49.

August 1950

All shapes and sizes

Col. Scott is urging everybody with any kind of dog to enter it in the comic dog race at 6 p.m. The laugh that the comic dog race raised last year was heard in Bradpole.

August 1950

The late Mr. Jack Pethen

A sad event has happened so quietly in Uploders that the parish has been almost unaware of it. Only two months ago Mr. Jack Pethen, nephew of Mrs. Samways, of Cherry Tree Cottage, was running a 200-acre farm near Horsham, and living with his parents. He was of very fine physique, and scarcely knew what illness was. He went to his doctor with what he thought was a minor complaint, and discovered that he was a desperately sick man. The farm had to be sold up, and the family moved to Uploders, where, in a short time, Mr.

Jack Pethen died. He was 43, and unmarried, an only son, with one widowed sister. His holidays had frequently been spent in Loders, where he was known as a sportsman and a good shot. The deepest sympathy will be felt with his parents, who are making their home in Uploders.

August 1950

The Clerk of the Weather

'Yf Crystemas Day on Monday be,
A grete wynter that year have shall ye,
And fulle of wyndes, lowde and stylle.'

So runs the prophecy of an old manuscript kept in the British Museum, and the present weather suggests that the prophet knew what he was talking about. But he was as liable to error as the B.B.C. weather forecasts, for he prophesies that if Christmas on a Sunday be, the summer following shall be 'fayre and drye'. It could not be inferred from the summer through which we have just waded that last Christmas did fall on a Sunday.

December 1950

Clammier than oysters

The deep sympathy of an area considerably bigger than Loders is with Miss Enid Allen, of Callington, in the sudden loss of her brother, Captain Roland Allen, R.N., at the age of 50. He will be a loss to the church, of which he was a councillor who worked hard at fêtes, and to the Agricultural Discussion Club, of which he had just been elected chairman. It was an achievement for a newcomer to farming to have won, in two years, the regard and affection of a band of Dorset farmers, who are thought to be clammier than oysters. It must be long since so many men attended a funeral in Loders Church. He had managed completely to regain his old cheerfulness in the short interval between his collapse at the farmers' meeting on the Friday, and his death in hospital on the Sunday.

December 1950

The Clerk of the Weather again

Spring is round the corner. (This we say well knowing that winter may yet be with us for weeks.) The morning light comes earlier, and the evening light stays later. The birds are singing at dawn, and the snowdrops are showing in the churchyard. Wise gardeners have been clearing their ground, and doing all the digging they can, to ease the work in March and April. At this time, when we are preparing to co-operate with nature in the bringing forth of new flowers, fruits and vegetables, the Church sets her season of Lent, which means 'Spring'. Her hope is that as we clean up our gardens, we may clean up our characters also, and that as we watch the buds bursting into leaf and blossom, we may ask whether the most important part of us, our soul, is also alive and growing. 'What shall it profit a man if he gain the whole world and lose his own soul?'

December 1951

Pulling their weight

Two members of our congregation who are Young Farmers made a weighty contribution to the success of their respective clubs at the Dorset County Rally. Miss Marjorie Randall collected 9½ points for her club, which was the best individual effort for the whole county, and beat the collective efforts of some of the competing clubs. Miss Sarah Barnes, of Dottery, won points for her club in the cheesemaking, and bids fair to be the champion young cheesemaker of Dorset. Few Young Farmers make cheese.

June 1951

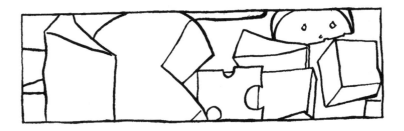

Farmers at the lectern

The Farm Service, like wine, improves with age. A large
congregation of farmers, young farmers, and agricultural
workers, came to Loders Church in a steady downpour of rain.
The rain was most welcome, but it kept at home the 'foot-
sloggers' who were coming from Powerstock, and Uploders
pedestrians. The hymns, all of them old favourites, were sung
with gusto, and the choir treated the congregation to an
anthem, beautifully sung. Part of the interest of this service is
to hear the lessons read by unfamiliar voices. To the readers,
their performance is an ordeal; for some of the congregation
there is sly pleasure in watching the victims go to the lectern;
and for the Vicar there is anxiety lest the reader should faint.
But this year's team were confident and clear, and acquitted
themselves nobly. The readers were Mr. H. Crabb, chairman
local Agricultural Worker's Union, Mr. C. Pitcher, chairman
Askerswell and District Young Farmers, and Mr. A.J. Wells,
vice-chairman Loders and District Agricultural Discussion
Club. We are grateful to Mr. Eades for lending us a plough to
put in the chancel, and to Mr. C. Pitcher for hauling it.

June 1951

The 'Hat trick'

The day of our Fête was gloriously fine, and the day following was abominably wet. This has happened for three years in
succession, which makes us think that the Clerk of the Weather
must have a soft spot for Loders Church. Never were two days
more unlike than the 21st and the 22nd July, 1951. The 21st
was a perfect summer's day. The lawn of Loders Court, with
its picturesque background of manor house and church, was
drenched in sunshine, and the tall thin trees were abuzz with
bees. It was the ideal day for the Fête. By contrast the 22nd
produced the worst thunderstorms of the year, and forked lightning caused deaths elsewhere in the south. In spite of the heat,
there were showers of hail-stones. Our fête workers looked out
of their windows, and thanked their lucky stars.

August 1951

The perils of agriculture

This year's haymaking at Upton will be remembered for the crop of accidents which marred it. One of the staff, Mr. Carver, caught his hand in a conveyor belt, and lost a thumb and a forefinger; Mr. Peter Morey also got caught in a belt, and was lucky to escape with no more than a wrenched arm; while Mr. Eli Lenthall twisted his ankle and had to take to crutches. To this chapter of accidents must be added mention of Mr. Bolton, who has been in Bridport hospital for some weeks, and is making progress.

August 1951

Wild flowers bedecked the grave

The most touching thing about the very impressive funeral of the Rector of neighbouring Symondsbury was that the children of the village school picked bunches of wild flowers and strewed them on the heap of earth beside the grave. They will sorely miss the somewhat fierce-looking patriarch whose visits to the school were welcome because of the goodies he used to bring with him.

August 1951

Harvest cigarettes

Differences in the weather distinguished Dottery Harvest Festival from Loders. At Loders the sun of a perfect autumn day streamed through the windows for matins, and the hunter's moon shone full through the east window for evensong. At Dottery it was a day of thunder, lightning and rain. Loders had almost a full church at matins, and a very full church at evensong. But Loders had the advantage of enticing weather. Dottery literally went through fire and water to prove its devotion to Harvest. The weather could scarcely have been worse, and yet there were few vacant seats when the congregation rose to sing 'Come, ye thankful people'. The preacher was hard put to compete with the rattle of rain on the tin roof, but a hearty 'We plough the fields and scatter' by the congregation quite subdued it. Both churches were beautifully decorated. At Loders a preponderance of sheaves seemed to have brought a cornfield right into church, and the Dottery dahlias made a florist's window of its baptistry. Those who guessed where the cigarettes came from that were among the Dottery gifts guessed right.

November 1951

When bees make mistakes

One gentleman in Loders who could raise no enthusiasm for harvest festival was Mr. Brake, of New Road. His principal crop is tobacco. He grows and cures enough to keep his own pipe going the whole year round, and usually there is enough over to test the stomachs of his best friends. But this year his crop is nil. He swears by all his household gods that he put in tobacco seed, and that tobacco plants came up, but that the bees muddled the process of pollination, and turned them into foxgloves. Mr. Brake thinks that the bees behaved scurvily. If they had to meddle with his tobacco plants, they might at least have turned them into Canterbury bells, as they are reported to have done for another tobacco grower up-country. Mr. Brake was taken aback to learn that he might have manufactured digitalis from his foxgloves, and cured all the bad hearts in New Road. Bees are knowing creatures. The foxgloves may have been intended as an antidote to Mr. Brake's tobacco. He, having smoked the tobacco for several years, the bees, in their wisdom, might have considered that a little digitalis was called for.

November 1951

Of farmers and dentists

Guests at our Young Farmer's Harvest Supper could not help thinking what a good thing these young farmer's clubs are, not just because they give the guests the most satisfying meal of the year, but because it is so good for young people to be active instead of passive in their leisure, making their own meal, their own plays and their own speeches. One agreed with Farmer White's admirable homily on punctuality – and was left wondering to what extent he had secured it in meetings of his own Farmers' Union. Any one who had seen the beautiful old farm smocks that had appeared on the stage that evening would ask, with Mr. Rolf Gardiner, why, at the County Harvest Festival in Salisbury Cathedral, the farmers who processed to the altar with their gifts had to be wearing dentist's coats. Surely the point that we are living in the Health Service Age need not be pressed thus far?

December 1951

Christmas cards – Easter weather

Christmas cards on our mantlepieces looked ill at ease this time. They were offering us the usual expanses of snow, and frosted twigs, while we were preferring the spring-like sunshine that the unpredictable English climate was lavishing upon us. The Christmas-card robin seemed positively annoyed not to be the only bird about, for the air was throbbing with bird music. When the flag of St. George mounted the top of his pole on Loders tower, he thought it was Easter, and skipped like the psalmist's ram. Worshippers made an airy morning walk of the long path down to church. They remarked, toughly, that the weather wasn't a bit like Christmas – and thanked God that it wasn't.

January 1952

Church mice

These are proverbially poor and thin, but the seven which Mrs. Wensley has lately caught in Dottery Church were fat and well favoured. They feed on chrysanthemums. The Chinese do, too, only they fry their chrysanthemums in batter. Our mice help theirs down with candle. Candles being the price they are, it is fortunate for the Dottery exchequer that Mrs. Wensley is so good a mouser.

January 1952

One pair of lungs

A Dottery christening, which brought a large congregation to church, was that of the infant son of Mr. & Mrs. Mudford (née Margaret Harris). It was the first grandchild of Mr. Harris, of Bilshay, and needs must that he be brought to the font of his forebears. Organ, congregation and parson together were no match for his one pair of lungs.

February 1952

From boots to shoes

Uploders has lost its picturesque and efficient cobbler, Mr. Tudball, [see page 103] who has just gone into retirement at Waytown, Netherbury. He came to Uploders in 1932, but he has been cobbling for 68 years. The very day he started has not slipped his memory. It was a fourth of February, and the big difference between cobbling then and now is that there were no shoes to cobble when he began: both women and men wore boots. One would think that at 84 Mr. Tudball had earned a rest. But no, he hopes to dig half an acre of garden and keep pigs and fowls. It hurts him to part with Uploders people because (he says) they are a 'nice lot'.

March 1952

The answer lies in the soil

Farm Sunday, which is our own pet name for Rogation Sunday, falls on May 18th. The farm service at Loders Church has become an institution. Discussion Club, Young Farmers and Agricultural Workers attend in state, and a plough is put in the chancel as a reminder that life depends on agriculture, and God's yearly miracle of growth.

May 1952

On his perch

The weathercock is back to duty on Loders church tower. He looks much improved by his long holiday. His plumage is now buttercup yellow, and the fiery red of his comb, unlike the naughty twinkle in his eye, is quite visible from the grass beneath. We have Mr. Charlie Gale to thank for his recuperation. One gale took him away. Another put him back. O.K.?

May 1952

Footing it

With fine contempt for the townsman's habit of queuing for ten minutes for a bus to take him ten yards, some people walked from Nine Bottles, in Askerswell, to the farm service in Loders Church. Others walked from Pymore and Powerstock. The congregation was one of the biggest, and surely the

singing was the heartiest Loders has heard. The choir were in
fine fettle, and the congregation were quick to respond. The
lesson readers also did their part well. We are indebted to Mr.
Wilfred Crabb for the loan of the old horse plough, and to Mr.
Clifford Pitcher for hauling it to and from church.

June 1952

Promoted to glory

The funeral of the late Rector of Askerswell, Canon Daniell,
took place at Litton in a setting which he, as a lover of the
countryside, would have liked. It was a perfect May morning.
The church seemed to be as full of flowers as it was of robed
clergy and mourners, and his moss-lined grave beneath the
towering trees of the churchyard was studded with bluebells.
Many of his old parishioners from Askerswell were present.
They took with them two large wreaths, one from the church
council and the other from the school children. The flowers
had been collected from the gardens of Askerswell, and skilfully made up by Mrs. Fooks.

June 1952

Cutting it short

The story is told that the shortest service the late Canon Daniell conducted in Askerswell Church was on a summer afternoon when a member of the congregation told him that bees were swarming on a shrub in the churchyard. The Canon was a great bee-keeper. He got through the service in record time, and was over to Litton Rectory and back again with the apparatus for collecting a swarm, at a speed not usually connected with dignitaries of the Church. The bees swarmed again the other Sunday night, during evensong. This time they were on the eaves of the nave roof, above the pulpit. The sermon was cut short on this occasion, not by the urgent desire of the preacher to collect a swarm, but by his anxiety to avoid it. Bees were invading the pulpit before he left it.

June 1952

The Jackdaw of Askerswell

At the top of the spiral staircase in Askerswell tower are two bushels of sticks, blocking the doorway to the roof. On the sticks sat a jackdaw. Between her and the sticks were three baby jackdaws. When the Rector's face appeared at nest level, she flew at him, and forced him down the steps. Possible, in his dark suit, she took him for a trespassing rook. Days later, when the faces of Mr. Studley and Mr. George Bryan appeared at nest level, she fled in a flurry of feathers. It would be interesting to know what she thought they were.

July 1952

Death-watch beetle

When the contractors who are re-opening Loders Church got
to the tower roof, they found that the timbers supporting the
lead were all rotten, and that the vibration of the bells was
likely to bring down the entire roof. Water seeping through the
perished lead had softened the oak timbers and made food of
them for the death-watch beetle. The timbers of the priests'
room were also completely rotten, and so were parts of the
nave roof. It was impossible to gauge the condition of the roof
timbers before the lead covering had been taken up, and in
consequence we find that the architect's estimate of £100 for
new timbers is inadequate. He tells us that we shall be lucky
if the receipts for the lead cover the cost of the new roof.

August 1952

A full programme

In this year's Fête, at Loders Court, on Saturday 2nd August,
an effort has been made to meet the old complaint that
there is not much to see or do. The children are coming in
fancy dress, and their dancing will include a minuet in
period dress. At 6.30 p.m. there will be slow bicycle racing,
jousting, sheep dog demonstrations, square dancing and a
sketch by the Women's Institute. There is no reason why
anybody should not be pleasantly occupied from early
afternoon till night-fall. Competitors in the flower show
have been occupied for weeks in trying to ensure that their
exhibits shall be at their best on the show day. Gardeners
declare that a carrot is harder to bring to perfection than a
Dorset Down.

August 1952

Young Farmers double success

Askerswell and District Y.F.C. came back from the County Rally at Dorchester with two coveted trophies – the Gardening Loving Cup for the best harvest supper, and the cup for the best stage entertainment. This gives them points towards a new seventy guinea cup for efficiency presented by a cattle cake firm. Mr. Clifford Pitcher must be feeling mighty proud of his club, and Miss Sarah Barnes is probably consoling herself that it was no disgrace for Beaminster to be beaten by a club like Askerswell.

January 1953

Typically English

For two years in succession Loders Discussion Club have listened to Mr. 'Bunny' Lenthall, the noted Dorset sheep-breeder, argue with passionate conviction that 'sheep are essential to the modern farm'. They have voted unanimously that he is right, and last month it was in the face of forceful arguments by Mr. Gilks to the contrary. Yet, as far as we know, nobody in these two years has acted on Mr. Lenthall's advice. They vote that sheep are essential, and still do not keep them. Substitute church for sheep, and man for farm, and the voting – and the consequent inaction – would be the same.

February 1953

Tempus fugit

To the writer of these *Notes* it seems odd that he should have come to the task of preparing his readers' minds for Easter when he has only just finished thinking about Christmas. These sunny days of March, some of them as warm as the normal English summer, make the anticipation of Easter even odder. One looks up at the rooks, whose nests are nearly finished, and down upon gardens, already dug and planted, and finds it hard to believe that Good Friday is yet to come. Good Friday is associated in many rustic minds with the breaking of the first sod in a winter-bound garden. There are worse ways of keeping Good Friday than digging, for the first round of digging is painful, and may be a reminder that Good Friday is the memorial of the most painful thing that ever happened – when the world crucified its God and Saviour. Right-minded people can never make a gala day of Good Friday. In one sense it is a triumphal day. The world's salvation was won on that day. The ancient poet looks at the Cross with perceiving eye and exclaims, 'Christ is reigning from the Tree, O tree of glory, tree most fair, ordained those holy limbs to bear'. But the price paid on the Cross humbles and subdues rather than elates a righ-minded person. The day for elation is Easter. This is the day that proves what thinking people had always suspected, that good is bound to triumph over bad, and that death is not the end of a good life. Old Mother Church gives us the chance of coming early to the Sepulchre to meet the risen Christ, through the Communion service. Every confirmed parishioner is bidden to make Communion on Easter Day. Nothing is lovelier than to see whole families kneeling at the altar rail in a church converted by spring flowers – and by the Real Presence – into Joseph of Arimathea's garden.

April 1953

Of weeds and table skittles

A Loders character has passed from us by the death of Mr. Sidney Marsh. He was a model of industry and thrift. Until a long and painful illness put him to bed he had scarcely stopped work, which was his hobby. Like his father and his grandfather before him, he was a market-gardener, and there was truth in the local saying that no weed could live where Sidney was. His large expanse of garden was as neat in dead of winter as in spring. By temperament he could hardly be called a clubable man, but his precisely measured visits to the local inn were always welcome. There his opinion on gardening matters was received like an oracle, and his prudence in withdrawing from table skittles at his first forfeit did not go unnoted.

May 1953

Of mice and men

Askerswell organ is being heavily attacked by mice. Food appears to be the motive. The palate for meat is now so universally corrupt that mice cannot tell what is meat and what isn't, with sad consequences for the organ bellows. However, there is no cause for undue alarm. Mr. Adams (for whose experience in the Cavalry we may now be thankful) has the situation in hand. A notice pinned to the organ proclaims that parts of it are poisonous, and that there are booby traps in others is obvious to those who know a 'Little Nipper' when they see one. It is another cause for thankfulness that the organist, Mr. Harold Spiller, is not allergic to mice, as he is to the jackdaws in the belfry. Indeed, this affront to Music has made him positively bloodthirsty.

May 1953

Leave it to the moon

Before leaving the subject of Easter, we would like to know what the advocates of a fixed Easter are thinking now. They want Easter fixed on the first or second Sunday in April. They think that by fixing Easter they can ensure fine weather. Let them ponder hard facts. This year the Sundays in March were much finer than the first two Sundays in April. That is the way of English weather. We know that putting the summer holiday in August is not proof against a bank holiday deluge. We may be better off by leaving it to the moon to fix Easter, as she has done from time immemorial.

May 1953

Of runner beans and marquees

The wedding of Mr. Guy Bryan, of Askerswell, and Miss Ann Doble, of Wootton Fitzpaine, robs Askerswell of a promising young farmer, who is making his home near Charmouth. That the bride's father regards Guy as a highly suitable son-in-law is to be inferred from his allowing the marquee which housed the wedding reception to be erected over his fully cropped kitchen garden. Some of the farmer guests could scarcely bring themselves to tread on the carpet when they knew there were potatoes beneath, but Mr. Doble did not mind as long as they were not treading on his runner beans, which the marquee had only missed by inches.

June 1953

Coronation babies

Three babies have recently been born in Uploders and Dottery. Had their timing been faultless, they might have all arrived on Coronation Day, and made Uploders front page news. The happy mothers are Mrs. Irons, of Uploders, who has a son, Mrs. Frank Powell, of Dottery, who also has a son, and Mrs. Smith, of Dottery, who has a daughter, which gives her family a nice balance of three daughters and three sons.

June 1953

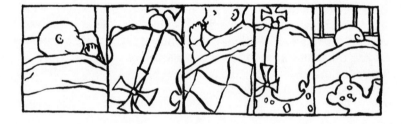

CHAPTER 7

Gentlemen, officers, foreigners

At home and abroad

The Reverend Oliver Willmott was appointed Vicar of Loders and Dottery by the Lord of the Manor of Loders, Colonel Sir Edward Le Breton, in 1947. (In 1952 he was appointed Rector of Askerswell as well.) The appointments may well have been sealed by his Army background. He was Chaplain to the Honourable Artillery Company during the Second World War. Subsequently, Vicarage and Manor became locked in a union that produced much that was fertile in terms of village life. The Court peacocks roamed the Vicarage gardens; the Vicarage children roamed the Court attics; the Court gardeners helped maintain the lovely borders of the churchyard path.

On one memorable weekend, some officers of the Honourable Artillery Company took up residence at the Vicarage. They wandered the ancient forest of Powerstock Common in pursuit of Sir Edward's pheasants and game. Next day, they were in their pew in the chancel in full regalia, and sobriety, alongside the Lord of the Manor and his Lady.

Lady Le Breton at other times was a stupendous provider of tea and cakes for the non-military, of every class and description. She also made sizeable anonymous donations to such causes as the church heating. Everyone knew that it was she who had done it. She was a Lady. Sir Edward later introduced the Vicarage children to television, particularly 'The Lone Ranger', 'Andy-Pandy' and 'The 6–5 Special', a revolutionary pop programme beyond Lady Le Breton's sphere.

The Court continued to be the setting for the yearly Fête. It grew in impetus, and profit, during the Vicar's time. Sherry for the carol-singers, and the annual children's Christmas party, with oranges and half crowns and Punch and Judy, became part of the sweet fabric of village life. Sir Edward welcomed scouts to his park in the summer, with lots of ceremony, and burnt sausages. In the winter, he let the lads of Bradpole – a fairly wild bunch from foreign parts two miles away – have the freedom of his billiard-table. The present Vicar of Loders, the Reverend Gregory Page-Turner, was surprised to find the line in the hymn 'All things bright and beautiful' about the rich man in his castle and the poor man at his gate still included. But a local widow in the congregation said, even in the 1990s, that it would be to 'upset the nat'ral order of things' to cut it out. The Court was the centre for the 'natural order'.

There was the occasional disruption to this idyllic harmony in the rural squirearchy. The Vicar would christen such an event a 'brawl'. He would pursue it to the bitter end, particularly the end of the churchyard wall. This leans gently, but still stands now, despite the professional predictions of Sir Edward's architect forty years ago. There is no doubt that it will stand well beyond the Millenium – it was the longest 'brawl'.

Only hints of these antipathies can be detected in the *Parish Notes*. They record faithfully the fruitful partnership of manor, vicarage, school (and pub). The Vicar was always gracious to those in defeat, and he was always certain that he himself had not been defeated. He had a penchant for people of elevated background, whether social, academic, or in connection with the services, or business. He had an omnivorous interest in all who visited his parish. He maintained contact with those who left, particularly those who continued to read (and pay for) the *Parish Notes*.

This chapter demonstrates his aristocratic leanings, his admiration for high-flyers, and his enthusiasm for real characters from foreign parts. Whilst being a great patriot (and monarchist), he was fascinated by the movements and concerns of ex-patriates – a sort of 'insider outsider'. His eye was finally on the whole of his flock, at home and abroad, and he only really admired aristocratic souls, from what ever class. But let the man speak!

Personalia

'Happyknowle', the home of Mr. and Mrs. Oscar Gale, has been living up to its name. Mr. and Mrs. Gale had a large and jolly party to celebrate the coming of age of their twin sons, Albert and Alfred. Albert is lately home from Palestine – to his parents' great relief. Alfred is now working away from home, to the regret of the Ringers, of whom he was a regular and very useful member.

July 1948

New parishioners

We are told that the population of Loders is in a state of continual flux. The most recent arrivals are Mr. Bob Newbury and his sister, at Uploders Farm, and Captain Allen R.N., his mother and his sister, at Callington. We hope they may put out roots, and stay. Mr. Newbury caught the eye of the B.B.C., and of the national press, by moving his stock by train from Northamptonshire, where he had been burnt out of an old farm of monastic origin. He has been a victim of four fires in eleven years, and looks to

Loders to change his luck. The arrival of Captain Allen has upset the balance of power at the Matravers end of the parish. The Army, in Colonel Dennis, is now outweighted by the Navy, in Commander Streatfield and Captain Allen.

August 1948

Loders born and bred

The late Mr. Fred Crabb, of Watercleaves, came of an old Loders family. The native families are not so numerous as one would expect. His father was the local road contractor, with whom he worked until the Great War. He was exempted from military service on medical grounds, and went to work at Upton Manor, where he remained for nearly 30 years. Upton Manor casts a spell over its old employees. Shortly before his death, Mr. Crabb said it would break his heart to leave Upton.

September 1948

English idyll

If any overseas tourist happened to be among the crowd at the wedding of Miss Heather Osborne to Mr. E.J. Pavey, he must have gone back with an idyllic picture of English village life. The flowers along the path to the church were in their glory, and the flowers in the chancel were no anti-climax. The interest shewn in this wedding was an indirect compliment to the bride's mother, whose public-spiritedness is almost a proverb in Loders. No deserving cause seeks her services in vain.

October 1948

Manor grandchildren

Sir Edward and Lady Le Breton are still rejoicing in the birth of a son, Edward Francis, to their daughter Mrs. Laskey. Mother and baby have returned from London to Loders Court. To be widely known is not all honey. Mrs. Laskey has about 100 congratulatory letters and 60 telegrams to answer. The letters included three from the families of former Vicars of Loders – the Palmers, the Beardmores and the Huttons.

November 1948

Old campaigner

Mr. and Mrs. Harry Sanders have had their grandson and his parents staying with them, from Scotland. He is their first grandchild and is now four months old. His father has the distinction of having taken part in all the invasions of the last war, and holds seven campaign medals.

November 1948

Return of a native

Mr. Frank Crabb, son of Mr. & Mrs. W.G. Crabb, of Loders, is home from Canada for the first time since he went there 18 years ago. He manages a ranch, and lives near his brother William, who migrated before him. Mr. Crabb says there is no danger of his overstaying his leave. The shock of having to exist on 2/11d worth of rations ensured that.

December 1948

Parish party

The answer to the oft-repeated question, 'When is the parish party?' is January 13th, at 7.30, in the Ex-Service Men's Hut. Socials seem to go down better than whist drives or dances. They provide a bit of something for everybody. There will be prizes for adult and children's fancy dress, as last year, and the ubiquitous Commander Streatfield has to come from the back-o'-beyond to be M.C. He hopes to bring a naval entertainer with him. Commander Streatfield's heart is always in Loders. The Vicar would never be surprised to receive a cable from Timbuctoo, saying that the Commander regretted his inability to attend the Church Council. A telegram of apology once came from him in Oxford.

January 1949

The Navy Lark

Able-Seaman Oscar Symes was married to Miss D.L. Samways at Allington on Dec.18th. He is the third youngest of Loders' longest family, originally eleven children. He likes the Navy, and has signed on for twelve years.

January 1949

Working party, Loders style

Who put the idea into their heads, we do not know – possibly Sir Stafford Cripps – but the girls of our Bible Class asked if they might run a working party among themselves, to make articles for their missionary sale next Christmas. The result is that ten girls now meet at the Vicarage on Saturday afternoons. Jessie Crabb & Margaret Barnes are teaching them to make toys, and articles of clothing, and already the finished work is rolling off the production lines. Jessie Crabb could find a ready use for any unwanted wool, or material.

February 1949

Master Laskey and Mr. Bevin

When the clergy of the Bridport Rural Deanery met in Loders Church on March 16th, they were much affected by the thought that the decoration of the church had been done in honour of their visit. But in fact, the decoration had been done for Master Edward Francis Le Breton Laskey, who had been brought to the font on the previous Saturday. The bad weather did not deter the muster of a good congregation for the christening, and it made all the more welcome the free refreshment offered in the inns of the village that night at the expense of the Lord of the Manor. Master Laskey sailed to New York with Mr. Bevin, which seems to mark him out for a career in diplomacy.

April 1949

Up from Down Under

Mrs. Palmer, wife of the previous Vicar, has come by air from New Zealand for a few months holiday in England. She paid a brief visit to to Loders Church, and called at the Vicarage and the Court. Both she and Rev. Palmer are enjoying better health.

May 1949

Lovers of the army

Mr. & Mrs. H. Sanders' soldier son, William, who is serving in Malaya, has been made a sergeant. He likes the Army. After his demobilisation he joined up again, for five years. Another keen soldier is Lieut. Donald Scott, second son of Colonel and Mrs. Scott. He is serving with the Scots Greys, and was one of the eight who represented the British Army of the Rhine at Henley.

July 1949

Sure evidence

The scene is a church in Canada, after Sunday morning service. The churchwardens are counting the collection. Among all the notes and the silver they see a solitary penny. They are surprised. 'Hullo, Tom,' says one to the other. 'Somebody from the Old Country at church this morning.'

August 1949

Former Lord of the Manor bereaved

A visitor from Cheltenham says that Mr. H. Ker Colville, of Sandywell Park, has been bereaved of his wife, which follows on the loss of his only child. Those who knew the former Lord of the Manor will be sorry to hear this.

August 1949

Thanks from a 'Small Person'

The day after the Gymkhana, Miss Juliet Williams, daughter of Sir Philip Williams, wrote Lady Le Breton a letter which said: 'Thank you so very much for doing all you did to give everyone such a wonderful time at the Gymkhana yesterday.

It was such a jolly affair, and I am quite sure that most of the smaller people, such as myself, with only one pony, and not a very good one at that, enjoy your gymkhana much more than the very large shows. Everyone is so friendly and willing to help.'

September 1949

In the time of the great Dr. Edersheim

Mrs. Mosely and her brother, Mr. Guppy, came over from Dorchester for Dottery Harvest. They are cousins of Mr. Cleal. Mrs. Mosely had not been in Dottery Church since 1898. She well remembers when there was no church at Dottery. As a girl, she collected for the building of Dottery Church, when the great Dr. Edersheim was Vicar of Loders. Mrs. Mosely is now 82. She has been married sixty years.

October 1949

The obsequies of Mrs. Scott

It must be a long time since the old walls of Loders Church can have looked at anything more poignant than the obsequies of the late Mrs. Scott. She had died in Edinburgh, while on holiday, and the service at the crematorium had been conducted by the Dean of Edinburgh. The casket containing the ashes was brought back to Loders, and put in the Easter Sepulchre, in the chancel, for the night. Early on the morning of the funeral her family attended Communion Service (how we wish more bereaved families would ask for this!). The casket was banked with flowers, and two lighted candles were before it. The family knelt nearby, and the potent words of the service seemed to dissolve the thin partition between this world and the other. A large congregation assembled for the funeral in the afternoon. The mother's casket was borne out of church by her two sons, Ian and Donald. Ian is a medical student, who was then on the very eve of his final examination, and Donald is a Guards officer, who had been fetched off manoeuvres in Germany. The casket was buried beside the path down which she had come so regularly to matins.

November 1949

From South Africa to Loders – back from the Dominions

It was pleasant to receive a call at the Vicarage from Mr. Harry Crabb and his daughter, of South Africa. He was a Pymore lad, and a member of that considerable band of locals who have made good in the Dominions. Mr. Crabb served his time in the navy, and then went to South Africa twenty-one years ago, where he now owns a flourishing motor business. His holiday in England has lasted some months, and has been spent in touring in a 'super' car – a small boy's nearest approach to the beatific vision. Mrs. Crabb would not leave the warmth of this car to risk pneumonia in the vicarage, but her daughter would. The daughter's re-action to the handsome Tudor fireplace, which is the glory of the Vicarage, was to ask whether we wouldn't prefer something 'nattier'. Certainly we would not. Mr. Crabb is a brother of Miss Minnie Crabb, of

Loders, who stayed with him for a time in South Africa. He has three daughters, two of whom are married.

November 1949

Fighting bishop

Our new Bishop, Dr. William Anderson, made his first official appearance in this Deanery when he instituted the new Vicar of Bothenhampton a few days ago. His fatherly manner, his fine voice, his suggestion of strength and stability, impressed us. He will be in continuous need of the two latter qualities if he is to stand up to the duties of a modern bishop, which have killed fine men ere now. Bishop Lunt had been a soldier bishop, winning the Military Cross in the Great War. Dr. Anderson is a sailor bishop, though he served as a combatant in the First King Edward's Horse in the Great War. In 1917 he was awarded the D.S.O. for action against enemy submarines.

November 1949

Obituary

At matins on November 20th the congregation had the unusual experience of hearing tribute paid to the memory of no less than three deceased persons. The first was Mrs. Rice-Oxley senior, who had died at Worthing. When in Loders she had been very regular at church, and was certainly the oldest member of the congregation. The second was Mr. W.V. Townsend, of Uploders, a veteran of the Great War, and for many years an invalid who had been a shining example of fortitude. The third was Mrs. Allen, of Callington, widow of the Rev. Reginald Allen, British Chaplain in Smyrna. She was highly esteemed by the Loders people who knew her. Her advanced age did not prevent her doing a big share of household chores – she seemed to get satisfaction out of it.

December 1949

Boer War veterans

Our notion that Captain Welstead and Mr. Clark are the only remaining Boer War veterans in Loders is wrong. There is a third – Mr. Tom Ward, of Yondover, who served in both Boer Wars. Mr. Ward is not as keen to put up his age now as he was then.

January 1950

Five generations

By the recent birth of a son to Mrs. Peckham Junior, a fifth generation was added to the family of Mr. Peckham, who succeeds Mr. Gillard as butler at the Court. The new baby has a grandmother, a great grandmother, and a great great grandmother, all very much alive!

January 1950

A date for Dottery

The memorial tablet to the Dottery men who died in the two world wars has been made, and is ready for fixing. It will be unveiled at 6.30 p.m. on Sunday, February 19th, by Colonel D. Scott, who will also give the address. It is appropriate that Col. Scott should do this. He served in the two world wars which the tablet commemorates.

February 1950

Gratitude where it is due

Lately, a bill for nearly £15 came in, for replacing the fan in the organ blower. This is more than our church collections produce in month, and to have taken £15 from the offertory account would have badly unbalanced it. Thoughts turned, as they always do on such occasions, to the free-will offering fund, and the bill was paid out of that. Last year, new hymn books for choir and congregation were needed, and the bill of £9 was paid from the same fund. This fund is our widow's cruze. It never fails us. We take it for granted, and are not a bit curious about the mystery of its replenishment. The time has come to acknowledge the debt of gratitude we owe to Lady Le Breton, and Captain Welstead, who are the only subscribers to the fund. It was they who paid for the new hymn books, and the new fan. A practical show of gratitude would be to give the valiant two a hand by saving up our collection when we are not at church, and dropping it in the free-will offering box when we are passing the church.

March 1950

Ex-naval commander

Commander Streatfield has been invalided out of the Navy. Probably this is regretted by the Navy as much as anybody, for he was obviously a 'coming' man. He has now turned his energy to food production, and is at present learning farming in Worcestershire.

April 1950

With flying colours to Southern Rhodesia

Mr. Tony Chard, of Loders, has long had an ambition to be a pilot. He went recently to Hornchurch under the National Service scheme and passed all the medical and written tests, thus becoming a cadet pilot. He was to have gone immediately for training in Southern Rhodesia, but is being held back for another draft.

April 1950

Spreading their wings

Mr. Stanley Diment and family have been spending the last few days with his mother in Loders. He, his wife, and two children, are about to sail for Australia. By trade he is a mechanic, but he means to try his hand at farming. He sees no future for an enterprising man in England. He hopes to be met at Sydney by the Williams, late of Spyway, who are now well established in Australia.

April 1950

Son of Loders

A young Australian was looking over Loders Church the other day. He said that his surname was Loder and that his ancestors had once lived in the Court. There is no record of a family of that name having held the Manor of Loders, but Mr. John Crabb, now aged 85, an authority on local history, recollects that we once had a policeman whose name was Loder, but he operated from Bradpole.

April 1950

Passion Play at Oberammergau

Mr. Ian Scott, elder son of Colonel Scott, has lately obtained the degrees of Bachelor of Medicine and Bachelor of Surgery of the University of London and is now a fully qualified doctor. Both he and Miss Alison Scott have joined a caravan party which is making for the Passion Play at Oberammergau, in the Bavarian Alps.

June 1950

Of bishops and their wives dropping in

The Bishop of Salisbury, Dr. Anderson, has lately done a pilgrimage on foot through the Wareham Deanery, preaching on village greens, putting up for the night at country parsonages and meeting his people in their homes. His wife, Mrs. Anderson, has been in this Deanery. She stayed a night at Mappercombe, and called on the vicars of Toller, Powerstock, Loders, Bradpole and Allington. She was charmed by Loders Church, where she recommended a new east window and figures of St. Mary Magdalene and St. George to fill the two empty niches in the Ladye Chapel.

The Bishop of Sherborne, Bishop Key, ever a lover of Loders, dropped in to tea on the Vicarage lawn on a recent Sunday afternoon.

Mrs. Lunt, widow of the previous Bishop, addressed the Deanery meeting of the Mothers' Union in Powerstock Church. Our own branch was well represented.

August 1950

Thoughts about the Fête

We can look back on our Gymkhana and Fête with satisfaction. For the fourth year in succession we had a fine day. At midday there were a few drops of rain, and these may have accounted for the longer time than usual that the Gymkhana took to 'warm up', but warm up it did. Our friends in neighbouring parishes supported us in strength. The Symondsbury contingent brought a diocesan bishop in the person of Dr. Vernon Smith, Bishop of Leicester. He is a cousin of Commander Streatfield. Symondsbury seemed grateful for the air of respectability that his lordship gave them. The children noted with satisfaction that in the matter of ice-cream the Bishop was a man of like passions with them, and that his enthusiasm for Punch and Judy was the equal, at least, of theirs.

September 1950

A lone furrow

Tribute ought to be paid here to the very hard work that some members of the congregation put into the Fête, and space forbids it, yet mention must be made of Colonel Scott, who bore the weight of the Gymkhana. For days before the event his solitary figure was to be seen against the bigness of the park, hacking at a beech tree which had fallen across the course. When a mountain of firewood indicated that his job was completed, he took a scythe, and groomed the entire course.

September 1950

From Vancouver to Dottery

We welcome to the parish Mrs. Rolston, late of Vancouver, Canada, who is busy settling in at Number Five, Dottery. She has lived for half her life in Canada. In the spring she had the misfortune to lose her husband. She has a daughter and a son. The daughter is married and living in New York; the son is in the Royal Navy and is stationed in Belfast.

September 1950

A Mothers' Union occasion

The Mothers' Union assembled in the Lady Chapel in strength for the induction of their new Enroling Member, Mrs. E. Lenthall, who had been elected to that office some months previously. Mrs. Minnie Crabb was at the organ for the first time, and the members were surprised to find they had an organist of such talent in their ranks for so long without knowing it. After service they adjourned to the dining room of the Court, where they found a tea of the quality that only Lady Le Breton can seem to command. She was warmly thanked for her hospitality.

November 1950

Lady Le Breton's largesse

A handsome donation of £60 has been made by Lady Le Breton towards the cost of repairing the boundary walls of the Vicarage. She may not be pleased to see this in print, but the parish ought to know how cheerfully she steps forward and shoulders parish responsibilities. It is not widely known that she gave the entire sum in the church heating fund, which now amounts to £240, and which awaits the licence of the Ministry of Works before it be expended on its object.

November 1950

The submarine *Maidstone*

P.C. Edrich is also in Bridport Hospital for observation. He is delighted by the discovery that Mr. Bengree, of Uploders, served with him on the submarine *Maidstone* during the war.

December 1950

Canadian connections

The family of Mrs. M.A. Budden, had their Christmas
saddened by her passing away a few days before the festival,
and further saddened by the inability of her daughter Marjorie,
who was sailing from Canada, to reach her before she died.
Mrs. Budden was something of an institution in Loders. She
had kept the village post office for years, and was known to a
generation of children as a dispenser of sweets who could
generally be depended upon to pity an empty pocket. She
brought up a large family, and worked hard. She was laid to
rest on her late husband, in Loders churchyard. Mrs. Minnie
Crabb was at the organ for the funeral service.

January 1951

A shock for Loders

The news that the 19-year-old flying officer son of Mr. and
Mrs. C. Chard had been killed in an air crash in Rhodesia
came as a personal blow to everybody in Loders who had
followed the career of this promising lad. The deepest sympathy is felt for his parents in the loss of their only child, and
for his fiancée, Miss Wyatt, who so often partnered him in
exhibition dancing at parish socials.

March 1951

Pilot Officer Cadet Tony Chard

The size of the congregation that attended the memorial service
of the late Pilot Officer Cadet Tony Chard left no doubt of the
esteem in which he was held, or of the measure of sympathy felt
for his parents. The Air Force have sent Mr. and Mrs. Chard
photographs and a detailed account of Tony's funeral in
Rhodesia. In this sad affair the Air Force have shown a niceness
of feeling which one does not look for in the war machine.

April 1951

New lands beyond the seas

Mr. and Mrs. Pearce have left Yondover to live with their children in Florida, and so increased the number of Loders folk

who have exchanged their native village for new lands beyond
the seas.

Of ten gallon hats

Mr. John Pearce, late of Yondover, and now of Florida, writes
that his wife and he are now happily settled with their daughter – after a 'very trying' voyage. They apologise for being too
worn out to say many goodbyes in Loders. The postscript says,
'They have already dressed me up in American clothes.' What
a pity that Loders should never see Mr. Pearce's portly figure
crowned by a ten gallon hat!

Hub of the universe

We are lucky in having Loders Court for big functions, and occu-
pants who are as ready to help us as Sir Edward and Lady Le
Breton. We hope they will survive the ordeal of being the hub of
the universe three times this summer. The Fête and the
Gymkhana will be at the Court by their kind consent, and so will
the Summer Rally of the M.U. branches of the Bridport Rural
Deanery, on June 21st. Add to that the usual invasion of scouts in
August, and it is clear that Loders Court is not as far from the
madding crowd as its position on the map might suggest.

Beating Sir Philip Colfox

The miniature flower show, was a most successful experiment.
It attracted some sixty entries of high quality. In the vegetable
class, Mr. Fred Taylor had the satisfaction of beating Sir Philip
Colfox. To the treasurer it was gratifying that the flower show
paid its way *and* contributed to the funds. Flower shows are
notoriously insolvent.

Outposts of the empire

Mrs. Martha Crabb's cottage in Loders has been one of the Focal points of the Empire this summer. Some of her many relations and friends who live abroad have been visiting her. A niece from New Zealand met a friend from Australia in her parlour, and they were followed by a friend from South Africa and another from Canada. Mrs. Crabb has eight nephews and nieces in Australia, a nephew in Ohio and another in Cyprus.

September 1951

Act of God on Long Island

Mrs. Laskey, daughter of Sir Edward and Lady Le Breton, has had an alarming experience at her flat in Long Island, New York. In a storm at night lightning struck the roof and set it on fire. The roof was well alight before the fire was discovered, and Mrs. Laskey had to escape barefoot, with her son Edward in her arms. She is full of praise for the local fire service, which is manned by unpaid volunteers. Within ten minutes of the call they were on the spot, bringing with them canvas shelters into which they put the salvaged furniture. Local builders replaced the roof and made the flat habitable in less than three weeks.

September 1951

Family reunion

Mr. & Mrs. Harry Sanders, of Loders, are relieved to have their son home, safe and sound, after three years of active service in Malaya. He is Sergt. William Sanders, of the 1st Battalion, King's Own Yorkshire Light Infantry. He was mentioned in despatches in Malaya. Until the age of eighteen he was a gardener at Loders Court, but he likes the Army, and is now a regular. His battalion is due for Germany in the near future. By a fortunate coincidence, his sister May was home from Scotland during his leave.

November 1951

Every dog has his day

The limelight at the wedding of Miss Alison Scott and Captain
Chater in Loders Church was stolen by her black Alsatian dog,
Atom. The local press seemed to have eyes for nothing but his
collar, tie and spats. One suspects that the beautiful attire of bride
and bridesmaids, and the floral decorations, were lost on the
reporters. But a photographer's eye was caught, and justly so, by
our veteran Captain Welstead, in tails and topper, being the very
outfit that he wore at his own wedding, but now with every button
doing its duty. The bridegroom knows the way to a ringer's heart.
He put five gallons of ale to the credit of our Ringers, at the
Loders Arms. Being on the credit side of Mine Host's slate so
excited them that they were still ringing at 7.30 on the morning
after the wedding. The adventures of the honeymoon began at
Dorchester, when a threat of fire under the bonnet of the car
turned out to be a kippered herring frying incontinently on a hot
pipe. They ended with an unfortunate tumble in the snows of
Austria, and damage to the bride's ankle. It's an ill wind,
however ... The bride is back in Loders for a few weeks, and
we have the benefit of her contralto voice in the Choir.

February 1952

Funeral of King George VI

Loders had a connection with the Royal funeral in Sir Edward
Le Breton. As a member of the Corps of Gentlemen-at-Arms he
did guard duty in Westminster Hall and at Windsor. He
performed a similar office for King George V, and was one of
the cadet guard which lined the Mall for the funeral of Queen
Victoria. He missed the funeral of King Edward VII by being in
India. Seeing him immediately on his return from the funeral of
King George VI, a person of peccable manners might have
remarked that some physical strain attaches to the wearing of
the uniform of the Gentleman-at-Arms for sixteen hours a day.

March 1952

'Hospitalisation'

As Chaplain of the Bridport Hospitals, Canon Clare used to
declare that always every other patient was from Loders. Last

month he was not far wrong, for there were five Loders people
in hospital – Mr. Brown the road contractor, Mrs. Lane, Mrs.
Slade, Miss Pearce and Miss Avril Greening. Mrs. Lane is
home, having recovered from a dislocated shoulder, and the
others are making good progress. The one who does not take
kindly to what the Americans call 'hospitalisation' is Mr.
Brown.

March 1952

Why not?

The news that the Vicar is a Z Reservist, and is about to be
called up for fifteen days' training, has evoked surprise, and
expressions of sympathy. But it is something to be thankful for
that the fighting services look on the Church as integral to
their scheme of things, and give the shepherds facilities for
being with the sheep. If the training is fifteen days of idleness
and boredom for the lay Z Reservist, it is anything but that for
the Army Chaplain. He is expected to give a half hour's talk
on Christianity, followed by a half hour of answering questions, to four different companies of men each day, and on the
Sundays to take services at camps scattered over a big area. It
really is good of the Army thus to put the youth of the country
in touch with the Church. We must pray that the best use may
be made of the opportunity. The Vicar's only grouse is that
this heavy programme of missionary work comes on top of
Easter. He goes to a camp in North Wales on Easter Monday,
and begins work the following day. Time alone will tell
whether the Vicarage ladies can be trusted to cover up the
early potatoes on frosty nights, and valet the sitting hens.

April 1952

Of Z reservists and lawn-mowing

The question that greeted the Vicar's return from military duty
was not as often 'How did you like it?' as 'Did they cover up
the potatoes and valet the sitting hens?' 'They' certainly did
her stuff. 'They' was midwife to three goslings and ten
ducklings; 'they' not only nursed the early potatoes but dutch-
hoed the garden, and distempered half of the Vicarage. His

Reverence was not at all displeased with 'They'. He tried not
to notice that the lawn was up for mowing.

May 1952

In triplicate

Three new babies have arrived since the last *Notes*. Our duty
herewith to the daughter of Mr. & Mrs. Laskey (grand-daugh-
ter of Sir Edward and Lady Le Breton), to the son of Mr. and
Mrs. Harold Brown, and to the daughter of Mr. and Mrs. F.
Record. The infant son of Commander and Mrs. John
Streatfield was recently baptised in Loders Church, the Rev.
B.N. Carver officiating in the absence of the Vicar.

May 1952

A surprise for both

A few weeks ago, when the nights were dark, Mr. Adams
answered a knock on his front door at Folly Cottage. The time
was after ten. Mr. Adams at once recognised the caller as the
Bishop of Salisbury, Dr. Anderson, and, to the credit of the
Bishop's memory, he at once recognised Mr. Adams. The
Bishop had been Mr. Adams' sergeant in their Army days. The
purpose of this unwitting call on Mr. Adams was that the
Bishop had lost his way to Powerstock. The Bishop has the
rare distinction of having been a sergeant in the Army, having
won the D.S.O. in the Navy, and having obtained a pilot's
certificate in the R.A.F., before he was ordained. He will be
holding a Confirmation at Loders in October.

June 1952

Rev. Charles Palmer

The late Vicar of Loders, the Rev. Charles Palmer, died on
17th July, in Auckland, New Zealand.

Miss Ruth Palmer had been helping Mrs. Palmer in nursing
him through a long illness.

August 1952

Loders–Malaya–North Africa

Dr. Ian Scott is now in the Army. He is with a Field
Ambulance, bound for Malaya. We shall miss him from the
Loders matins, and our best wishes will go with him. Lieut.
Donald Scott is almost recovered from a long illness, and is
fretting to join his unit in North Africa.

August 1952

Loders–Southern Rhodesia

July 22nd was a significant date for two Loders households.
Mrs. Green presented her husband with twins, a boy and a
girl, each tipping the scales round the seven pound mark; and
a daughter Helen Mary, was born to Mrs. Tom Pitcher's son
and his wife in Salisbury, Southern Rhodesia. Mrs. Pitcher is
a devoted grandmother, and this happy event seems to have
helped her recovery from a long illness. Mrs. Greening is
proud to have been elevated so decisively to the rank of grandmother.

September 1952

Bereavement at Askers

Much sympathy was felt for Mrs. Block in the death of her
mother, Mrs. Ada Watkin, who had been living with her. Mrs.
Watkin was 83. Her late husband was a sea captain of the old
type, and was drowned at sea. Mrs. Watkin was cremated at
Weymouth, and the ashes scattered in the sea off Portland.

September 1952

Death in paradise

Mr. John Pearce, who left Yondover to live with his children
in Florida, did not enjoy that paradise of film stars for long.
He died suddenly, while playing with his grandchildren. Mr.
Linee senior, lately on the staff of Loders Court, has also died,
at Didcot. He was a great sufferer.

September 1952

A distinguished visitor

On a Sunday in January the morning congregation at Loders included the Dean of Winchester, Dr. Selwyn, classical scholar and eminent theologian. Like that other scholar, Dr. Johnson, he has an affection for English inns, and during his holiday in Bridport he put up at The Bull. When the Vicar heard that the Dean was coming to service at Loders, the absurdity of his preaching to so great a divine hit him with force, and he placed himself with the congregation at the Dean's feet. But the big guns of the Church are not so easily fired (as witness, in another sense, the Dean of Canterbury). The Dean declined the pulpit on the unassailable ground that this was his first holiday since September (1952). On the day following it was made evident that the great can be very simple and homely when they choose. The Dean came to Askerswell church to baptise the infant son of Wing.Com. and Mrs. Newall, who are old friends of his. He had the small sisters of the neophyte standing on either side of the font holding lighted candles, and he called their elder brother from the pew to blow them out. As a father of four, the Dean is not unused to children.

February 1953

All aboard

Commander and Mrs. Streatfield are soon moving from Matravers to Broadoak. They will leave a big gap in the Church Council, and the family pew beneath the pulpit will be conspicuously empty because it was so often full. The friendly atmosphere which newcomers find in Loders Church probably had much to do with the Commander, whose jeep would start from Matravers on Sunday mornings, assume that every pedestrian between there and the Farmers Arms was bound for church, and take them aboard. The Commander's charm of manner was such that his passengers never had the heart to tell him where they meant to go. Besides, he was always careful to run them home again, but not before he had made tender inquiry among the worshippers who linger at the church gates, and encouraged them to keep their chins up. We shall miss our John Streatfield and family.

March 1953

A seat in the Mall

The Coronation seat allocated to Loders Women's Institute was balloted for by six members willing to pay the £4 for it, and was drawn by Mrs. George Bryan. Being in the Mall, the seat promises an excellent view, and Mrs. Bryan will not be harrassed by the thought of having to report the Coronation to the next meeting of the W.I., who have already extracted the promise of a report from Sir Edward. As a member of the Queen's bodyguard, his view will be as good as any.

April 1953

From rubber-planting to West Dorset

Capt. and Mrs. Mason have taken the bungalow recently vacated by Mr. Dick Nantes. They are no strangers to West Dorset. They once lived at Morecombelake, and Capt. Mason's uncle was Vicar of Allington. Capt. Mason finds Askerswell a welcome change from rubber-planting in Malaya.

June 1953

Congratulations to Sir Edward Le Breton

We take it upon ourselves to offer the congratulations of Loders to Sir Edward Le Breton on his receiving the M.V.O. in the Coronation Honours list. By a coincidence he will be coming direct from the Queen's Investiture to give his talk on the Coronation to this month's meeting of the W.I.

July 1953

CHAPTER 8

The parish pump

The price of fish at West Bay

The Vicar was voraciously interested in village affairs. He was always walking around, talking with people, noticing things. Though he had his aristocratic leanings, he was keen to hear the gripes and groans and genuine concerns of all mortals. He had his finger on the pulse of the villages. He steered a diplomatic path between the interests of most men, and most women. In reality, the dilapidated pump opposite the school in Loders was perhaps not such a significant place as the Pound next to the Old Cottage, opposite the Post Office. In the past, stray cows and sheep were herded there. But people know what kind of affairs are discussed around the Parish Pump: the school, the Young Farmers, the price of mackerel at West Bay, not to mention a few more sensational matters.

The end of this book focuses on the Coronation of Queen Elizabeth II in June 1953. Before then, you will have heard of exciting matters such as 'The Parish Council that made history'; the

extraordinary tale of the uninsured horse at the Gymkhana; and
the unfortunate soul who had two graves dug in different places –
and others. But there is one word which springs from these
unrandom jottings from a country parson, and that is
'Community'. There was great pride in the children of the village.
Their education and entertainment were cared for in equal
measure. Everyone knew each other, and everything was recorded
– even 21st birthdays, or 'Comings of Age'. Everyone had a place
and was accepted, despite animosities which may have existed at
garden-fence level. At the Pump, literally and metaphorically,
was the Vicar, who was the humble centre of his self-found
universe. He knew everybody in it. And most things.

Loders School

In 1869 Dame Isabel Nepean built an Elementary School for the
parish. Loders was lucky, for most parishes had to build their own
school by public subscription. In accepting the use of the school
the parish promised to keep it in repair. But for many years past
the parish has not spent a penny on its school. The Board of
Education now insists that the school building be brought up to
the required standard. If Loders is to keep its school, the
managers must produce a substantial sum for repairs by the end
of this year. Hence, the Gymkhana and Fête in the Park on
Saturday, July 31st. We hope this may raise enough to secure the
school. The parish is rightly convinced that the policy of shutting
village schools is detrimental to the countryside. The Fête gives
us a chance to convert conviction into action.

July 1948

Something to suit all fancies

Given fine weather, July 31st should be a red letter day. There is
something to suit all fancies – jumble stalls and the like for housewives seeking bargains, sports for the children, skittles and
sideshows for the competitive, dancing for young men and
maidens, and the Gymkhana for everybody. The Fête begins at 2,
and the Gymkhana at 2.30. The Fête committee was in a dilemma
over prices of admission. The usual charge for a Gymkhana is
2/6d., but parishioners who had already contributed to the stalls

could not be expected to pay that amount. So parishioners – and parishioners only – are asked to enter the park by the main Court gate, for which the charge will be a shilling. Non-parishioners will enter by the gate opposite Yellow Lane, for two shillings.

July 1948

Folk-dancing on the Vicarage lawn

Miss Wilkes, Governess of Loders School, will be away on July 31st, so the children's display of folk-dancing, which was to have been at the Fête, will be on the Vicarage lawn instead on Thursday, July 22nd, at 3. Parents, and all interested in the school, will be welcome.

July 1948

Vicar's letter

My dear Parishioners – on the Sunday after the Gymkhana and Fête I thanked the parish for making the event such a success. The aim of this letter is to extend the thanks to those who did not hear me in church. I am still rather dazed by your achievement, and people in other parishes raised their eyebrows, too, when they read how little Loders, population 638, and practically all working people, had raised £157 for their village school. If asked to account for it, I would say that (a) the village school, and the mistress who has served it so well and for so long, have a strong hold on village sentiment; (b) what the church workers of Loders lack in numbers they more than make up for in energy; (c) Loders people are generous – cottagers who could produce nothing for the stalls gave sizeable cash donations instead; (d) Loders people are good-humoured – if they opened their door to a different stall collector five times in one day, they only laughed, and sent the collector on her way rejoicing; (e) the weather was kind. I noted again how lucky Loders is to have Dottery inside its ecclesiastical boundaries. Dottery is not served by Loders School, but Dottery ran a profitable stall, several competitions, and supplied much needed man-power on the gate. I trust Loders may be as loyal to Dottery when any need arises up there. – Yours faithfully, O.L.Willmott, Vicar.

September 1948

Collecting the fourth coach

The Sunday School Outing to Bournemouth was delayed an hour in starting, while a fourth coach was being fetched, to cope with the unexpectedly large company of trippers. The fine weather had decided many waverers at the last minute, and the Vicar had taken a chance which did not come off – he had not cycled to Dottery the previous evening and checked their final numbers. Fortunately for him, people are used to inconvenience these days, and this seemed but a trifle to the trippers. The day was a happy one. The party numbered over 120, and their ages ranged from a few months to well over 80 years. It was much regretted that the Elliott family, staunchest supporters of the Sunday School, could not join the Outing. Mary had gone down with chickenpox only three days previously.

September 1948

Monday night at seven

The Women's Institute has arranged through the County Council to hold leatherwork classes in the School on Monday evenings at 7 o'clock, beginning on September 12th. Leatherwork is an interesting hobby, and may be made quite profitable too. The course of eight lessons costs 2/6d. and is open to all. Miss Butterworth, of 25, Loders, would like names and fees as soon as possible.

September 1948

Invading hikers

New guide-books are now to be had in Loders Church. The high cost of printing has doubled the price to 1/- each. Five of the first 25 books put out were stolen, a loss of 5/- to Church funds. The traditional honesty of Dorset folk is not in question. The culprits were hikers, who must have been invaders.

October 1948

Golden wedding

Mr. and Mrs. W.J. Elliott, of Yondover, are shy, and are trying to keep secret, without much success, their golden wedding which occurred on September 8th. May we add our congratulations to the many they have received? Mr.& Mrs.Elliott are the proud, and the revered, heads of a family of 7 children, 28 grandchildren, and 10 great-grandchildren. Family feeling among the Elliotts is strong and healthy, and the whole clan came to pay their respects on, or near, the anniversary.

November 1948

Light entertainment

Employees of the Brit Works are doing two sketches for the Choir Party in the Hut on Thursday, Dec. 16th. The Choir have planned to give the village a very jolly evening. There will be songs, dancing, games, refreshments, and devices not to be disclosed, all for 2/- (children half price).

December 1948

Eminent ladies' dignity

The social life of Loders needed some keeping pace with in December. There was something 'on' almost every night – dances, whist drives, socials, then, nearer Christmas, carol singing and private parties. This is all to the good. We want the village to have a vigorous life of its own, and not to be a mere dormitory of Bridport. Our male population is envious of the lucky gentlemen who saw the Women's Institute in the relaxed mood of their mutton and lamb party. By all accounts, nothing funnier has been seen since Mr. Oscar Gale appeared as Old Mother Riley at the Victory celebration. Regard for the dignity of certain eminent ladies precludes details.

January 1949

Behind the scenes

The Choir Social owes some of its success to Messrs. David Crabb, Clem Poole, & Harry Sanders. An hour before the social, it was discovered that the piano ordered from Bridport had not arrived. These three did a strong man act in getting a fine but heavy instrument of Mrs. Laskey's down awkward back stairs at the Court. Mr. Edgar Bishop drove it in a trailer to the Hut. Then there would have been no coloured lights on the Christmas tree in the chancel but for Mr. Follet. He did in an hour what others had spent a whole morning in trying to do – make them light.

January 1949

Legal ham

The profit on the parish party was £10. 16s. 0d. Takings were £16 and expenses were £5. 4s. 0d. Some of the refreshments, and certainly the most delectable, were given – as usual, by the handful of generous people who never fail to turn up trumps when Loders is on pleasure bent – but the party was very large, and food had to be bought. Believe it or not, some people are troubled lest the ham they ate at the party might have been eaten illegally! It is unlike Loders to be sensitive to the nice points of the Law, but so like Loders not to have doubts before the ham was digested. Tender consciences should be relieved to know, on the authority of the Bridport Food Office, that the giving away of one's own ham, killed under permit, does not offend the Law. So that particular road to gaol is closed to our genial People's Warden.

February 1949

The last of the season

Our most successful series of parish socials will end with a mid-Lent Social at the Hut on Thursday, March 24, at 7.30 p.m. It is designed to give the parish some relief from the rigours of Lent, and to pay off the £17 outstanding on the school roof.

March 1949

To the parents of children under five years

We earnestly hope that when your child reaches the age of five, you will choose to send him to our own village school. If the number of pupils in any school falls below a certain level, the school cannot hope to be kept open. Our own school has a very limited population upon which to draw, and needs support. In the year ended March 31st, 1949, some £200 will have been raised by Loders people for the improvement of their school. Where will be the logic of this, if, at the same time, they condemn their school to death by not using it? Local patriotism, and a desire for the fulness of village life, are not the only basis of our appeal. There are sound educational reasons for supporting a school like ours. Education proper begins at the age of eleven. The business of a primary school is not to fill a child with fancy knowledge, but to give him the tools for his education, which are, reading, writing, arithmetic, and discipline. Children could have no better exponent of these than our own Miss Wilkes. She is a teacher of long experience and proved ability.

March 1949

Merrymaking under difficulties

Illness has lately touched most homes in the parish, though local patriots have it that our sufferings have been nothing like those of Askerswell and Shipton Gorge. The mid-Lent social was on that account most difficult to run. Widecombe Fair lost Mr. Drake to 'flu, and thereafter the producer. Mrs. E. Bishop, found herself with a different team at each rehearsal. The Misses Joan and Alison Scott had to make heroic efforts to get their Red Riding Hood ready. At the last minute the refreshment department lost Mrs. T. Hyde, who is the parish expert in coffee making – and was lucky to find a substitute in Mrs. J. B. Osborne, who bids fair to be another expert. But the unkindest out of all was dealt through Mr. Tulley. Instead of singing Widecombe Fair, and MC-ing the party in his own inimitable way, he followed the fun in spirit from a sick bed, and that could not have been easy under an attack like his. In spite of everything, we had a happy evening under the aegis of Mr. Charlie Gale, and the School Managers received a profit of £15 1s. 6d. for their roof. Mrs. Willmott takes this opportunity of thanking those who responded so generously to her appeal for refreshments. Mrs. Taylor also deserves our gratitude for doing her amusing monologue at short notice. The school roof should beam on Mr. Billy Darby every time he

goes by. His music contributed greatly to the success of the
three winter socials, and saved the heavy expense of hiring.

April 1949

Making history

For the first time that anybody remembers, Loders is to have
a contested election for its Parish Council. There are nine
candidates for seven seats. One wonders why there was never
a contest before. A reason may be that the cost of an election
falls on the rates, and canny parishioners were loth to add to
them. Another reason may be that parish councils are now
virtually stripped of their powers, and may seem scarcely
worth bothering about. But it is still to the advantage of a
parish to have a good council. We might not have had a new
surface to Yellow Lane, or a new bridge to Boarsbarrow, or a
telephone kiosk in Uploders, if the executive authorities hadn't
a Parish Council to harry them. The limitations of a parish
council are painfully clear in the matter of housing and of the
railway halt. The parish badly needs new cottages, but the allo-
cation of cottages is done by a higher authority, which cannot
be circumvented when it says that it must first build houses
where the need is greater than in Loders. Concerning the
railway halt, British Railways have had at their disposal for
several months a piece of ground which they have judged suitable; an energetic parish councillor has been writing to the
M.P., interviewing the Railways, phoning the Ministry of Town
and Country Planning; and the position to date is that British
Railways blame Town and Country Planning for the delay, and
T.C.P. hotly blames B.R. Now we know why in some parishes
there are no candidates at all for the council.

May 1949

Check mates

'Ye Game and Playe of Chesse' was the title of the first English
book ever printed. Will those who play chess, or who would
like to learn, please give their names to the Vicar? We have in
the parish an enthusiast who wants to arrange some play for
the winter evenings.

July 1949

A week of revelry

Are you proud of your old parish and priory church of Loders? You have reason to be. It never fails to arouse the admiration of visitors. Sunday, July 24th, in the octave of St. Mary Magdalene, is the one Sunday in the year set aside for thanking God for Loders Church. It is the Dedication Festival, and the church will be decorated with summer flowers. Between you and me, that is the day above others when the Vicar would like to see the faces of his friends and neighbours, the old Loders families – his own flock – at the services, as well as visitors. The visitors are always welcome; indeed, we depend on them, for quite half of our regular congregation are visitors; but it would be good, if only for once, to see the faces we know and like, in their own church. Dedication Festival is not a new-fangled idea of the Vicar's. It is as old as Loders. Have you heard of Loders Feast? If not, ask Mr. & Mrs. John Crabb and Mrs. Budden. They can tell you how, towards the end of July, there was always a week of revelry. Sweet stalls and shooting galleries were set up along the main street of Lower Loders, and on the Saturday night of the Feast, the biggest bedrooms of the Farmers' Arms and the Loders Arms were cleared of furniture, for dancing to the music of concertinas, tambourines and fiddles. Whether the revellers were conscious of it or not, they were celebrating St. Mary Magdalene, and rejoicing over the dedication of Loders Church. So turn out on the 24th as you would to Harvest!

July 1949

Orthodox taste

Our publicity agent would give his shirt to get the opening
ceremony done by Dick Barton, or some other hero of this
modern age, who would draw everybody within a twenty mile
radius to Loders, but the committee will have none of this.
They prefer to be orthodox, and to leave the opening ceremony
to the good taste of Lady Le Breton.

July 1949

A relic of Loders Feast

In her china cupboard, Mrs. John Crabb has an egg cup which
came off one of the stalls that used to be set up along the
village street for the week of Loders Feast, in honour of St.
Mary Magdalene.

August 1949

The distant city of Dorchester

Our congratulations to Mrs. Quarm (née Betty Poole) on the
birth of a daughter, are a month overdue. Betty now lives at
Dorchester, and it takes time for news of that distant city to
seep through to Loders. What might be interpreted as indif-
ference on the Editor's part was mere ignorance. He had not
'heard'.

August 1949

Improvements to the school

A bevy of expensive-looking cars, parked outside the school
one morning last month, piqued the curiosity of the entire
neighbourhood. They had brought the Assistant Director of
Education and his retinue for a consultation with the Managers
apropos of improvements to the school. As a result of this
meeting, plans are being made for an internal water supply
(hot and cold), and wash basins. This should make the school
canteen much easier to run.

August 1949

A school occasion

The Vicarage lawn, with the old house as a background, made a perfect setting for a display of folk-dancing, and acted nursery rhymes, by the children of our schools on a summery afternoon in July. They were watched by a numerous gathering of parents and friends, whose faces looked as happy as the children's. The guest of honour was Miss Garland, a former and much loved teacher, who, having taught under Miss Wilkes, the present governess, for twenty-one years, is now on the staff of St. Mary's School, Bridport. During an interval of speechmaking in which Miss Wilkes spoke warmly of Miss Garland's work in Loders School, Reggie Drake presented to Miss Garland a Revelation suitcase, which had been subscribed for by past and present pupils, and Caroline Elliott presented a posy. Miss Garland thanked the pupils, and said the suitcase was a welcome gift, for she had been about to buy one. Adding his tribute to Miss Garland's work, the Vicar spoke with regret of the approaching retirement of Miss Wilkes, and hoped, if this could not be postponed, that Miss Garland might come back as governess in her place, in which event this would not be the last presentation Miss Garland would receive from Loders School.

August 1949

Compliments

The Vicar would like to commend the efforts of the Agricultural Discussion Club, the Young Farmers, and the Women's Institute, to revive the corporate life of the village. Fresh in his mind is the visit of the Discussion Club to Litchfield Manor, the 2,000-acre estate of Major N.D. Wills. This was a day to remember – good lunch in Andover, tour by truck of rich Hampshire cornlands, halt for liquid refreshment, tastefully set out by the host, a barn of church-like proportions, and a sumptuous tea on the estate manager's lawn. Days like this make village life worth living, and we are gratified that the local originators of these three movements are loyal sons and daughters of Loders Church.

August 1949

Uninsured friend

The Gymkhana was marred by an accident which befell (is it necessary to say?) the Bishop family. It happened before the gymkhana. Joan was riding one horse, and leading another, and coming out of the farm on that awkward corner, when she was run into by a car, driven by one of the Colfox family. The horse, Jacob, which she was riding, was damaged beyond repair, and had to be destroyed. Joan, very fortunately, was unhurt, and it says much for her nerves that she was able to go on to the Gymkhana and compete. Jacob had been a friend of the family for eight years, and a winner of many prizes. Sympathisers who tried to soften the blow with words of comfort about a fat cheque from the insurance company were wide of the mark. Incredible as it may seem, there are still people who do not insure their friends.

September 1949

All's well that ends well

After all the differences of opinion as to where we should go for the Sunday School Outing, we embarked upon it gingerly, our spirits unimproved by the threat of a heavy thunderstorm. Yet it turned out to be the best outing we have had, and some children were moved, for the first time, to send 'thank you' letters to the Vicarage. By the time the three coaches put into Lyme, the weather was set fair, and at Seaton the sea was perfect for bathing. The coaches took the party to the Tower Café on the cliff overlooking Seaton for tea, which contained a surprise in the form of bowls of ice-cream, brought in when the feast was thought to be finished. At Beer the children watched the fishing boats unload, explored the smugglers' cave, and joined spontaneously in the General Thanksgiving when they were looking over the village church.

September 1949

Grave mistake

Our sympathy is with the husband and children of the late Mrs. Hetty Day, of 6, Pymore Terrace, who died suddenly at the early age of 55, and was buried at Dottery. We regret that a

grave was also dug at Loders Cemetery, through a misunderstanding. To prevent a recurrence of this, we would impress on
the Pymore people that the ecclesiastical parish of Loders, and
the civil parish of Loders, are not identical. Pymore is in the
ecclesiastical parish of Loders, but not in the civil parish, and
consequently residents of Pymore have no right of burial in the
civil cemetery at Loders. Their burial rights are in Dottery
churchyard.

October 1949

Bonny Prince Charles

Mrs. Barnes, of Bilshay Farm, represented our M.U. at the big
service in the Central Hall, London, which was addressed by
Princess Elizabeth. She regretted that she could not get near
enough to Prince Charles to bring back a first hand description of him for Loders mothers, but she brought a glowing
account of the meeting.

November 1949

Fire worship

The children of Loders got the kind permission of Mr. Burrell
to let off their fireworks round a bonfire on Waddon, on Nov.
5th. Mr. Ian Scott was firemaster. The guy had been made by
Mr. Wells. It took all the nerve of the ex-Gunnery Officer of
the *Vanguard* to look composed as things exploded and hissed
behind and beneath him. The whole company enjoyed it
immensely, and so did a full moon. Apples were devoured, and
in a fine frenzy the fire-dancers vowed a sacrifice of sausages
next year.

December 1949

Devoted service of the governess

Miss Wilkes' twenty one years as governess of Loders school
come to an official end on Sunday, April 30th, when she goes
to retirement in Bournemouth. So passes a faithful teacher in
the old tradition, who has trained two generations of Loders
children. These children (many of them are now grown up, and

she has taught their children) combined a wholesome fear of her stick with a genuine love of her person, and they are all sad at her departure. The whole village shares the regret. She recognised that the training of children is as sacred a calling as that of priest or nun, so she never quibbled about wages, hours and conditions, as modern teachers sometimes do. Indeed, she was always dipping into her own pocket for her children. When they left the School, she gave each girl a brooch and each boy a purse, or half-a-crown in lieu. It was she who bought the oranges and crackers at Christmas, and paid the children's fare to the Folk-Dance Festival at Bovington, and she regularly sent a treasury note, unasked, towards the Sunday School outing. The collecting book will soon be going round on her behalf. We want to give her something she will be able to prize to the end of her life as a token of Loders affection. The presentation will be made at the school at 3 o'clock on Friday, April 28th, 1950. Everybody will be welcome.

Presentation to Miss Wilkes

Friday, April 28th, was Miss Wilkes' last day as Governess of Loders School. Lessons ended at three in the afternoon. The children sat on the floor in a half moon round her desk, and behind them sat a big assembly of parents and old pupils. Miss Wilkes was at the desk, supported by Sir Edward and Lady Le Breton, and the Vicar and Mrs. Willmott. Sir Edward started the speech-making by thanking Miss Wilkes for her twenty-three years of devoted and highly efficient service to the school, and wished her every happiness in her retirement. This was echoed on behalf of the old pupils by Mrs. Pearl Symes. Mrs. Willmott then presented Miss Wilkes with an envelope containing £26. 1s. 6d., emphasising that it was the result of spontaneous giving by pupils, old pupils and friends, and not of a house-to-house collection. Mrs. Symes and Miss Jessie Crabb, two old pupils had acted as treasurer. On behalf of present pupils, Jennifer Paul handed to Miss Wilkes an exquisite bouquet, which had been made by Mrs.D. Crabb. The reply must have been something of an ordeal for Miss Wilkes, for by this time it had dawned on the children that they were losing their beloved teacher, and several were crying. She, however, braced herself like the departing schoolmaster in De Maupassant's *'La Dernière Classe'*, and reviewed her twenty-three years at the school. She thanked everybody, from Sir Edward, who had paid the managers' share of school repairs out of his own pocket, down to the school neighbours, Mr. & Mrs. John Crabb and Mrs. Burrell, who had passed pears, carrots and strawberries over the playground wall. She made a warm reference to Mrs. Darby, the caretaker, for her help with the school meals. She ended by saying that she hoped to buy a good watch with the money she had been given, and commended to the school Miss Barlow, her successor for the time being.

In a letter recently received at the Vicarage, Miss Wilkes says, 'I spent the day in Exeter last Thursday, which resulted in my becoming the possessor of a watch which Brufords assure me is the best which can be bought. It has a very clear neat dial, and, what I think will please the donors most, a gold case. The price was £18. 6. 5d. With the surplus money I propose to buy a very homely article, an electric blanket. Then I shall have a Loders watch to look at by day, and a Loders blanket to keep me warm by night. On looking through the list of donors, I find that so many of them have left Loders that I do not know their present addresses. As the *Parish Notes* travel far and wide, I wonder if they could include a notice of my thanks to the donors for their kindness and generosity?'

June 1950

The modest gardener

The death of Mr. G. Pritchard has left a void in the life of Uploders, where he was often seen, and seldom heard, but greatly liked. His cottage garden, with its array of flowers, was eloquent of his skill as a gardener, yet by birth he was a townsman, who began life in Reading. He started work in Huntly & Palmer's biscuit factory. Then he entered the service of the Arden family as a gardener, and remained in it for forty years. His garden produce was well up to exhibition standard, but he could never be persuaded to compete in shows. In his last illness he was nursed by his daughter and son-in-law, who had come from Egham, Surrey. His age was 76.

November 1950

Seasonal pastimes

The winter activities of the village have begun. The Agricultural Discussion Club started the new season with some
fifty members. Captain Allen's election to the chair holds a
promise of spicy meetings to come. Mr. R. Ascott is vice-
chairman, and Mr. Edgar Bishop secretary. The Women's
Institute is in the throes of a general election. Many candidates
have offered themselves for election, to the committee, thus
submitting their popularity to the acid test of a secret ballot.
The children's sewing party have begun their weekly meetings
at the vicarage. They are making articles for their Christmas
sale in aid of the church overseas.

November 1950

Merry mummers

It used to be part of the Christmas sports for villagers to put
on outlandish clothes and masks, and go mumming from one
neighbour's house to another, partaking of Christmas cheer.
The custom survived at Powerstock until modern times. The
Vicar has a faded photograph of the Powerstock mummers, and
some of them are still alive – very much so. In Loders the
mantle of the mummers has fallen on the Church Choir. They
sing carols through the village in the week before Christmas,
and partake of Christmas cheer where it is offered. But their
mumming has a philanthropic side: they carry a collecting box
for the C. of E. Children's Society. This Society is particularly
deserving of our support, for it has just taken a Loders child
under its wing.

December 1950

In sick bay

Mrs. Darby, caretaker of Loders School, and mother, for seven
hours a day, of all the children who attend it, is in Bridport
Hospital for observation and treatment. To rest and be waited
on makes her feel like the Queen of Sheeba, she says. The
children, impatient for her return, send her letters, and the tiny
tots send her drawings. Occasionally from the hospital there

comes a reply in Mrs. Darby's own hand, which is read out by
the governess at school opening, and listened to intently by the
children.

December 1950

A children's Christmas

Loders children say, with good reason, that they have had a
very happy Christmas. They got a free tea at their missionary
sale; they had another tea, and presents from Father Christmas
at their school breaking up party; at church on Christmas
morning they received packets of sweets from the Christmas
tree; at the Court on the last Saturday of the old year they had
the grandest party a child could wish for; and then the Junior
Choir were taken to the pantomime at Weymouth and given
tea. Even the County Council joined in the conspiracy to give
the children a good time. The school meals department sent,
at the end of term, an iced Christmas cake, and Christmas
puddings with sixpences in them. This was on the rates, of
course, but it is likely to be one of the few items of County
Council expenditure which nobody will begrudge.

January 1951

Book this date

There will be a parish party in the Hut on Tuesday, Jan. 30th
at 7.30 p.m. You are invited to come IN DISGUISE. There
will be a prize for the disguise which defies detection longest.

January 1951

Charades

The Woman's Institute Party in the Hut enlivened an otherwise
cold and miserable February evening. Bradpole W.I. were the
guests. They tended to enter all their heavy weights for the
competitions needing quickness of manoeuvre, which lost
them the races, but stoked up the fun. Miss Alison Scott is a
genius at producing amusing charades without much rehearsal.
Her team of performers blushed to hear her apologise to the
audience that the rehearsals had been 'not many'.

March 1951

Of netmaking, braiding and darts

Loders has been put in the news by some of its netmakers and
by the dart players of the Loders Arms. In the braiding competitions at the Bath and West Show, Mrs. Harry Legg and Mrs.
Rogers were first and third respectively in one class, and Mrs.
Chubb, of Dottery, was second in another. The Loders Arms
dart teams seem to have made darts history by winning two
cups simultaneously.

July 1951

Children's day

The children say that they thoroughly enjoyed themselves at
the Fête. There was much for them to do. They quickly discovered a children's stall where they could buy sweets off points,
and toys within the scope of their small purses. Within the
shade of the church was a huge supply of ice-cream, presided
over by a kind lady who was not too particular about payment.
Out in the wide open spaces, pony rides were to be had, but

the thing that pleased them most was the whirligig house. The sight of a queue of children waiting to go in (one child confesses to five rides in succession) must have rewarded the hours of skilful work that Mr. Arthur Linee had put into its construction. In their turn, the children gave much pleasure to the grown-ups by their country dancing, which was a credit to them and to their teacher, Mrs. Clark.

August 1951

There's lots of good fish in the sea

The Choir Outing was typical of the unity in diversity which characterises the members of the Choir. On a lovely summer evening they proceeded independently to Lyme Regis. Some made for the cinema to see Tom Brown's Schooldays, and the rest were for the harbour. There these collected a boatload of holiday-makers for a phlegmatic seaman who was bedding down his ancient craft for the night, and took him mackerel-fishing. He had said that mackerel were scarce, but the Choir and their newfound friends caught a bucketful. The other part of the Choir went from the cinema to an eating-house called the Nook, and dined with the propriety befitting the Choir; the mackerel-fishers sat them down in a tavern in the harbour and swelled the songs which were enlivening that quarter of the town. Later, the whole Choir, or nearly the whole of it, met by accident in the car park, voted that they had had a splendid outing, and then went home their several ways.

August 1951

The Clerk of the Weather again

The Gymkhana is on Saturday, September 1st, in the park of Loders Court. Adult riders will of course be welcomed, but it promises to be largely a children's show. The 'horsey' children of the neighbourhood are looking forward to it, and have even decided what events they are going to win. The same may be true of the dogs who are running in the comic dog race. Colonel and Miss Alison Scott are the organisers of the Gymkhana. Their eyes are anxiously on the weather, and they have in mind the liverish attitude of the Clerk of the Weather

to this season's equestrian events. It will soon be seen if he
still loves Loders.

September 1951

The boggy field

The Gymkhana was good for our souls. In previous years the
weather had always smiled on us, and we sometimes wondered
how we would face up to it if the weather frowned. Now we
know. Rain fell mercilessly most of the morning and afternoon, but the competitors turned up, some of them from a
distance, and 'the show must go on' became the order of the
day. The entries reached the surprising number of 87, and this
encourages the supposition that fine weather would have made
the day eminently successful. The cosiest spot on that boggy
field was Mrs. Harry Legg's tea emporium under the cedar
tree. There the sweetest smiles of herself and her bevy of lady
helpers atoned for the rain. The eyes of many customers turned
to her warm stove, but it could not be come at for the ice-
cream man, who seemed glued to it. Thanks to the handsome
profit on the teas, to a few donations, and to the kindness of
Mr. H.K. Barnes in doing the haulage gratis, Colonel Scott,
who has not quite finished his battle with the accounts, thinks
that the Gymkhana may just pay for itself, which is a relief to
himself more than anybody, he being chancellor of the
church's exchequer.

October 1951

Improvements to the hut

The Young Farmers and the Women's Institute, who are the most
frequent users of Loders Ex-Service Men's Hut (and therefore the
main source of its revenues) suggested to the Ex-Servicemen that
the Hut needed certain repairs, and to be made more comfortable.
The Ex-Service Men met to consider these proposals, and made
the agreeable discovery that their thrifty treasurer, Mr. Oscar
Gale, had amassed a credit balance of £217. The meeting
appointed a committee to recommend improvements costing not
more than £90. The committee consists of Messrs. O. Gale, W.
Symes, H. Legg, G. Hyde, E. Paul, C. Allsop, and the Vicar. It

met immediately after the general meeting, and decided to get estimates for two sets of outdoor steps, for curtains, and for stopping draughts. The history of the Hut reads like something out of Trollope. Local Ex-Servicemen built it themselves with their share of the canteen fund of the Great War. They were not careful to elucidate the ownership of the land on which they built, and it turned out to belong to a gentleman at Chideock. As the hut was standing on his land, the law held that the hut also belonged to him. With difficulty he was persuaded to sell the land to Sir Edward Le Breton, who let it to the Ex-Service Men on a 99-year lease. The presumption is that technically the hut belongs to Sir Edward.

October 1951

Home-made wedding

The wedding of Miss Jean Neave, of Boarsbarrow, and Mr. K.G. Day, came the Saturday after Harvest, but some of the Harvest decorations had survived and been added to, so that the church looked equally beautiful, in another style. There was a large congregation to sing the hymns. A pleasant feature of the wedding was that it was home made, and good. Between them the bride, her sister, and her mother, had made the dresses, the bouquet, the three-tiered cake, and the banquet. Of the banquet it may be said that the Forster Institute can never have housed an ampler or a jollier feast. It was a touch of old times.

November 1951

Sheep dogs at Loders Fête

Mr. White of Washingpool Farm, has kindly consented to bring his champion sheep dogs Lassie and Pam, to Loders Fête, on August 2nd. They will show what dogs can do with sheep. We hope we may also see them putting the ducks to bed, but this depends on whether the ducks, being Aylesburys, can keep out of the way of green peas between now and then. Mr. Sanctuary and his team of Square-dancers will also grace the fete, and so, we think, will the children of Loders School, who hope to do country dancing. In previous years the Fête has fizzled out at six o'clock, and given way to a dance in the hut. The plan this year is to have the fête in two parts – stalls, sideshows, flower show, children's fancy dress and dancing and teas in the afternoon; and sheep dog trials, Square-dancing display, slow bicycle racing and jousting from 7 p.m. onwards, all in the park of Loders Court.

June 1952

Flag on the sands

Loders Sunday School rather surprised themselves by choosing a perfect summer's day for their outing. They, and a large company of parents, went by coach to Weymouth. The beach was crowded, but Mrs. Willmott, with the assistance of Mr. George Hyde, had made a big flag, with 'Loders Sunday School' painted on it, and this, fluttering bravely over the sands, helped to keep the party together. Even so, one child managed to spend much of the day in the lost children's nursery, and two others kept the heart of a devoted mother palpitating while arduous search was being made.

October 1952

New school governess

Out of some forty applicants, the managers of Loders School chose Miss Barbara Bryan, of Askerswell, to be the new head teacher, succeeding Mrs. Clark. Miss Bryan comes with excellent testimonials, and with the blessing of the County Education Officer, from a large school in Blandford. She is no more a stranger to responsible posts than she is to us. During the war she was in charge of the A.T.S. [Auxiliary Territorial Service] who ran the signals department of Mr. Churchill's underground headquarters in Whitehall. Miss Bryan specialises in infant training, and the present assistant, Miss Wickham, holds an exceptional qualification for the teaching of juniors. The school should benefit from having teachers each in her own element.

October 1952

Jumble sale philosophy

Mrs. Aylmer and the ladies who ran the jumble sale for Askerswell church funds surprised themselves, and us certainly, by making a profit of nearly £42. When they hear the result, people say 'Amazing!', and it certainly is for so small a parish. The sale not only roped in the shekels, but was really pleasant, and the workers found it full of fun. The two gentlemen who in the morning, emptied Miss Edwards' pretty cottage of the jumble that had filled it nigh to suffocating, and took it in their cars to the school, christened themselves Northover and Gilbert [Bridport removal firm]. To see them battling shoulder to shoulder with ottomans and pouffs, nobody would think that Northover, staunch churchman and Kiplingite that he is, had recently given Gilbert a tithe of some stuff smuggled across the channel, only to be denounced by Gilbert from the pulpit, Gilbert having first pocketed the contraband. Such an interlude might have reduced the temperature as between ladies. Great lad, Northover! He might also have taken umbrage at the school – and he didn't – when he was staggering across the playground under a load of coal and kilner jars, and an early arrival, Mrs. Fooks (veteran of many jumble sales) complained, with the Nelson touch, that she did not see any of the workers stirring, and had come expecting to find them 'as busy as cats in a tripe shop'. By the afternoon all the workers had done their stuff, and the schoolroom had the seductive atmosphere of Woolworths. The tea arrangements shewed genius definitely not Woolworths. You could get strong tea at one buffet, weak at the other, and exactly to taste by filling your cup up with the required proportion from each. Miss Edwards, of the haberdashery, also had a bright idea. She used one of the many charming ladies of the choir as mannequin, so that the customers who bought the jumble were beguiled into thinking that it would look as nice on them as it did on her. But the master-stroke was Mrs. Aylmer's. When her jumble sale was over she sold its remains (quite profitably) to a jumble sale at Toller. Now we know: the brutes eat each other.

November 1952

Couldn't care less

Weddings are notoriously prone to accident. The bride may be very late, the bridegroom may have come without the banns certificate, the best man may have lost the ring, or the parson may be missing at the appointed time. To all these, Loders has added something new and entirely original. A couple called at the Vicarage on a Tuesday, and arranged to be married by licence in Loders Church on the following Saturday at eleven. They furnished the particulars required for the register, engaged the organist and chose hymns. On the Saturday morning the registers were written up ready for the service, extra flowers were put in the chancel, and the organist left his work at Chideock and was at Loders by 10.45. Eleven o'clock came, but nothing else did. At 11.45 Vicar, Verger, Organist and Registers were still waiting. The Vicar then went to the bride's home. The door was answered by the bride's brother, who seemed as puzzled by the situation as was the Vicar. However, it was soon elucidated, for a taxi drew up, and out of it got bride and bridegroom, well garnished with confetti. The bridegroom told the Vicar that they would not be troubling him, as they had changed their minds, and got married in the Registry Office. When the Vicar asked why he had not been told of the change of plan, the bride said, with an air of langour, 'We were very, very busy, and we really hadn't time.'

December 1952

Christmas parties

Schoolteachers and parents saw to it that the term ended with seasonal jollification. At Loders, a large Christmas tree given by Sir Edward Le Breton and fixed by Messrs. David Crabb and Horace Read, occupied the centre of the school room. Children, parents and school managers sat down to an uproarious Punch and Judy show, then adjourned to the inner schoolroom for a tea which delighted the eye and defeated the heartiest appetite. They returned to the tree, and while the arrival of Santa Claus was awaited a presentation of a book token and a bouquet was made to the assistant teacher, Miss

Wickham, who was leaving the school. Santa Claus arrived somewhat late. He had had trouble with his reindeer, but his sack of presents was intact, and these he distributed with a word of wisdom for each child. At Askerswell school Miss Wilkinson and her companions, known locally as 'The Ladies', amused the children with a programme of games, and conditioned them for a welcome issue of ice-cream. There followed a prodigious tea, prompting the remark, 'It is wonderful where the food comes from', and finally an exchange of presents. A few nights earlier, Askerswell School had seen another delightful party. The elder girls taking part in Miss Robinson's concert felt that she and Miss Edwards, who had made the costumes, and Miss Wilkinson, who had made the music, deserved an evening-out for their labours, so they roped in their friends, laid out an attractive supper on tables for four, and followed it up with a programme of games, each of which carried a delectable prize. The guests enjoyed themselves, and were full of admiration for the way in which the young hostesses carried the party through.

January 1953

Brownie revels

The Guides and Brownies of Askerswell have fresh and very pleasant memories of the Christmas parties that Miss Edwards gave them at her home. She shewed her genius in keeping a crowd actively amused within the confines of a cottage – even to a ritual dance round a toadstool. There was ingenuity also in her giving of presents, which had to be traced along beams of a giant spider's web to the remote corners of the house. Askerswell children are too genteel to admit that they appreciated the delicacies provided for tea, but they did.

February 1953

Not as bad as it looked

We were pleased to learn from Mrs. Taylor, of Uploders, that the press reports of her son Roy's accident were somewhat exaggerated. He is making a good recovery in Dorchester hospital, and expects to be home any day. As Loders knows,

Roy is a great pedal cyclist, who thinks nothing of cycling to
Paris. If the weather is not blowing a blizzard, he cycles to
Poole on Friday nights for a cup of coffee. He was going for
his coffee when this accident occurred. An overtaking car
dismounted him, and made a total wreck of the bike on which
he has covered so many thousands of miles.

March 1953

To celebrate a new monarch

Coronation plans are now taking shape. The Loders
Committee have received £56. 18s. at the time of writing
(collections, Uploders £20. 5s. 3d., Yondover £8, Loders
£13.17s. 6d., Whist Drive £14. 15s. 3d.) The Dottery collection, which is understood to be doing well, is not in yet, and
more is promised from Loders. Hopes are high concerning
the revenue-raising possibilities of Mr. Well's pig, which is
to be skittled for at the Hut on Easter Saturday and Easter
Monday. The Committee have been saved any expenditure on
Coronation jugs by the offer of Sir Edward and Lady Le
Breton to give one to every child in Loders and Dottery of
school age and under. The sum saved to the Committee may
be judged by the number of children eligible, which is in the
region of one hundred. It is proposed, subject to the approval
of the parish meetings, to make this the Coronation Day
programme:- Afternoon, Procession of children and adults in
fancy dress, and decorated vehicles, from Matravers to the
Court, followed by sports and tea at the Court. The evening
celebrations to centre on the Hut, and consisting of dancing,
items by Young Farmers, Women's Institute and Church
Choir, continuous buffet and bar, skittling at Wellplot, all
rounded off by bonfire and fireworks in Mr. Randall's field
in Knowle Lane. Houses to be decorated for competition,
children to be taken to the film of the Coronation in Bridport,
and pensioners and invalids to be given souvenir tins of tea
or biscuits. Coronation funds raised in Askerswell are nearing
£60, and there is more to come in. The Askerswell
programme was outlined in the last *Notes*. If there is any
money left over, Askerswell hopes to buy a new parish notice-
board, and seats for use in the school. This is not too ambi-

tious. Rumour has it that our neighbours in Bradpole were intent on using their surplus cash to put a clock in the church tower, until they found that the clock would cost £500.

April 1953

Eligible bobby

P.C. Edrich, who maintains law and order in Loders and Askerswell, has been successful in passing the Police Sergeants' examination, which makes him eligible for promotion. He was seventh on the list for all Dorset. In our own interests, we should not be sorry if the promotion were long delayed, for he tempers the sternness of the Law with courtesy of manner and cheerfulness of mien.

April 1953

Copies of the complete Parish Notes, 1948–1982, photocopied and bound in two volumes, may be obtained from the editor at:
8, Bishop Street, Shrewsbury SY2 5HA at a cost of £50, which includes packaging and postage. (Cheques to be made payable to The Bishop Street Press.)

The Parson from the prologue to the Canterbury Tales

৵ের৲

Geoffrey Chaucer (circa 1343–1400)

A good man was ther of religioun,
And was a povre PERSOUN of a toun;
But rich he was of holy thoght and werk,
He was also a lerned man, a clerk,
That Cristes gospel trewely wolde preche;
His parisshens devoutly wolde he teche.
Benigne he was, and wonder diligent,
And in adversitee ful pacient;
And swich he was y-preved ofte sythes.
Full looth were him to cursen for his tythes,
But rather wolde he yeven, out of doute,
Un-to his povre parisshen aboute
Of his offering, and eek of his substaunce.
Wyd was his parisshe, and houses fer a-sonder,
But he ne lafte nat, for reyn ne thonder,

In siknes nor in meschief, to visyte
The ferreste in his parisshe, much and lyte,
Up-on his feet, and in his hand a staf.
This noble ensample to his sheep he yaf,
That first he wroghte, and afterwards he taughte;
Out of the gospel he tho wordes caughte;
And this figure he added eek ther-to,
That if gold ruste, what shal iren do?
For if a preest be foul, on whom we truste,
No wonder is a lewed man to ruste;
And shame it is, if a preest take keep,
A shiten shepherde and a clene sheep.
                    text by W.W. Skeat World Classics 1905

(from a verse translation by David Wright)
And there was a good man, a religious.
He was the needy priest of a village,
But rich enough in saintly thought and work.
And educated, too, for he could read;
Would truly preach the word of Jesus Christ,
Devoutly teach the folk in his parish.
Kind was he, wonderfully diligent;
And in adversity most patient,
As many a time had been put to the test.
For unpaid tithes he'd not excommunicate,
For he would rather give, you may be sure,
From his own pocket to the parish poor;
Few were his needs, so frugally he lived.
Wide was his parish, with houses far asunder,
But he would not neglect, come rain or thunder,
Come sickness or adversity, to call
On the furthest of his parish, great or small;
Going on foot, and in his hand a staff.
This was the good example that he set:
He practised first what later he would teach.
Out of the gospel he took that precept;
And what's more, he could cite this saying too:
'If gold rust, then what will iron do?'
For if a priest be rotten, whom we trust,
No wonder if a layman comes to rust.
It's a shame to see (let every priest take note)
A shitten shepherd and a cleanly sheep.
                    translation by David Wright O.U.P. 1985.

300

Parish Notes: Loders, Dottery & Askerswell.   August 1974

The charge for admission to Loders Fête at Loders Court on Saturday August 3rd is tenpence for adults, and for children nothing. The present inflationary processes look to have gone into reverse here; for greater value is being offered for the same money. There will be a gymnastic display by the athletes from Portland; an entertainment by the handbell ringers; a punch and judy show; children's sports; and the other appurtenances of a country fête. Our kindly neighbour Mr. Romanes, the Dorchester eye surgeon, will again be bringing his steam traction engine for those rides beloved of the children. The Hon. Mrs. Alexander Hood will declare the fête open at 2 o'clock, and her husband will be conducting tours of the house and will doubtless be explaining to an attentive company the famous naval pictures. The main financial object of the fête will be to help pay for a new lead roof on the church tower and turret; which is going to be abominably expensive, but will be costlier still if the weather is allowed to damage further the underlying woodwork. There will be the usual stall for the repair fund of Dottery church; and a stall for the repairs to Loders village hall. In keeping with ancient custom, the Vicar will begin collecting for the stalls in Uploders on the morning of Monday July 29th, and it usually takes him till the following Friday afternoon to work through the parish. Anything saleable, or cash in lieu of that, is grist to his mill. Cakes, confectionery, groceries, garden produce, unwanted Christmas & birthday presents, lively white elephants and bottles (but no empties, please) will be specially welcome. He dislikes being a beggar for a week. It requires a treasure as priceless as Loders church to give him the relish.

The Prayer Group which emerged from our branch of the Mothers' Union will resume meetings, after its summer recess, at the Vicarage, on the third Thursday in September.

July this year has not been open-handed with the high summer weather that we crave. But she seems to have a soft spot for Askerswell. On the morning of the Sunday on which the village gardens were to be open for general public inspection she seemed bilious from a Saturday hangover. There was wind and rain, and the proud gardeners feared that all their titivating might have been in rain. However, by Sunday dinner time she was feeling better; in the afternoon she broke into a smile, which lasted into the evening. Next day, poor thing, she had an attack of Monday morning blues, with paroxysms of wind and rain, which made the gardeners of Askerswell glad for their good fortune rather than sorry for her. The gardens had been looking fine the previous afternoon, and had attracted some 250 visitors. This is where the esprit de corps of the Women's Institute counts; for this year the enterprise was in aid of local W.I funds, and a notice in the W.I journal had brought people from miles around. One batch came in a coach from the New Forest. Everybody liked the gardens, and the feel of the village; and the teas on offer in the village hall shared in the general appreciation. Many people visited the church as well. We hope for the benefit of their own churches they took the point when, exploring the churchyard, they found Captain Churchwarden Michael Lumby making use of his spell of guard duty by tidying up that glory hole of a tool shed. Takings of A profit of £57 took the W.I funds with a whoosh out of the red into the blue.

The Isard family of Uploders and the Cadmans of Bradpole had a field day at Loders font when the daughter and son of Mr. and Mrs. Keith Cadman (nee Isobelle Isard) were christened on July 7th. The names of the girl are Rachel Sarah, and of the boy Robert William.

The collecting boxes for the Church of England Children's Society, organised by Miss Muriel Randall, have yielded £19.74, for which the donors are warmly thanked by the Society.

The country weekend spent here by the ringers of St. Bartholomew's the Great in the City of London would appear to have been a ~~great~~ success, seeing that their clerical leader, the Reverend Brooke Lunn, sent a letter of thanks on behalf of them all, and then they all wrote individually. Kindly July weather filled their cup of joy to the brim as they nosed through the Dorset lanes to sample the bells of Netherbury, Stoke Abbot, Powerstock, Askerswell and Abbotsbury. At Powerstock they were welcomed by the Dean Rural. Dropping into The Crown in Uploders they savoured the royal hospitality of landlord Reg. Small and his lady, and were loth to leave. They would have been

PARISH NOTES: LODERS, DOTTERY AND ASKERSWELL   AUGUST 1974

The charge for admission to Loders Fete at Loders Court on Saturday August 3rd is
tenpence for adults, and for children nothing. The present inflationary processes
look to have gone into reverse here; for greater value is being offered for the same
money. There will be a gymnastic display by the athletes from Portland; an entertainment by the handbell ringers; a punch and judy show; children's sports; and the
other appurtenances of a country fete. Our kindly neighbour Mr. Romanes, the Dorchester
eye surgeon, will again be bringing his steam traction engine for those rides beloved
of the children. The Hon. Mrs. Alexander Hood will declare the fete open at 2 o'clock,
and her husband will be conducting tours of the house and will doubtlett be explaining
to an attentive company the famous naval pictures. The main financial object of the
fete will be to help pay for a new lead roof on the church tower and turret, which is
going to be abominably expensive, but will be costlier still if the weather is
allowed to damage further the underlying woodwork. There will be the usual stall for
the repair fund of Dottery church; and a stall for the repairs to Loders village hall.
In keeping with ancient custom, the Vicar will begin collecting for the stalls in
Uploders on the morning of Monday, July 29th, and it usually takes him till the following
Friday afternoon to work through the parish. Anything saleable, or cash in lieu of
that, is grist to his mill. Cakes, confectionery, groceries, garden produce, unwanted
Christmas and birthday presents, white elephants and bottles·(but no empties, please)
will be specially welcome. He dislikes being a beggar for a week. It requires a
treasure as priceless as Loders church to give him the volition.

The Prayer Group which emerged from our branch of the Mothers' Union will resume
meetings, after its summer recess, at the Vicarage, on the third Thursday in September.

July this year has not been open-handed with the high summer weather that we crave. But
she seems to have a soft spot for Askerswell. On the morning of the Sunday on which
the village gardens were to be open for general public inspection she seemed bilious from
a Saturday hangover. There was wind and rain, and the proud gardeners feared that all
their titivating might have been in vain. However, by Sunday dinner time she was feeling better; in the afternoon she broke into a smile, which lasted into the evening.
Next day, poor thing, she had an attack of Monday morning blues, with paroxysms of wind
and rain, which made the gardeners of Askerswell glad for their good fortune rather than
sorry for her. The gardens had been looking fine the previous afternoon, and had
attracted some 250 visitors. This is where the esprit de corps of the Womens' Institute counts; for this year the enterprise was in aid of local W.I. funds, and a notice
in the W.I. Journal had brought people from miles around. One batch came in a coach
from the New Forest. Everybody liked the gardens, and the feel of the village; and the
teas on offer in the village hall shared in the general appreciation. Many people
visited the church as well. We hope for the benefit of their own churches they took the
point when, exploring the churchyard, they found Captain Churchwarden Michael Lumby
making use of his spell of guard duty by tidying up that glory hole of a tool shed. A
profit of £57 took the W.I. funds with a whoosh out of the red into the blue.

The Ward family of Uploders and the Cadmans of Bradpole had a field day at Loders
font when the daughter and son of Mr. and Mrs. Keith Cadman (nee Isobelle Ward) were
christened on July 7th. The names of the girl are Rachel Sarah, and of the boy, Robert
William.

The Collecting Boxes for the Church of England Children's Society, organised by Miss
Muriel Randall, have yielded £19.74, for which the donors are warmly thanked by the
Society.

The country weekend spent here by the ringers of St. Bartholomew the Great in the City
of London would appear to have been a success, seeing that their clerical leader, the
Reverend Brooke Lunn, sent a letter of thanks on behalf of them all, and then they all
wrote individually. Kindly July weather filled their cup of joy to the brim as they
nosed through the Dorset lanes to sample the bells of Netherbury, Stoke Abbott, Powerstock, Askerswell and Abbotsbury. At Powerstock they were welcomed by the Dean Rural.
Dropping into the Crown in Uploders they savoured the royal hospitality of Landlord,
Reg Small and his Lady, and were loth to leave. They would have been unable to leave
Rose Cottage had not their self control been equal to the flow of Mrs. Harry Crabb's
dandelion wine. On each of the two evenings the day ended pleasantly round the
capacious dining table of Loders vicarage. The ringers were too full and too tired to
be aware of the deficiencies of their makeshift beds, some of them in Chuck Willmott's
attic workshop. At Loders their ringing began on the Saturday morning, and at Loders
it ended with a farewell flourish to the congregation as they were streaming out of
Matins on Sunday. The ringers had a good journey back to London. That evening they
were ringing for evensong, finding perhaps that the powerful numinous atmosphere of the
Norman apse of the priory church of St. Bartholomew the Great was all the more wonderful for comparison with the light and graceful chancel of the priory church of St.

Priors and Vicars of Loders Church and Priory

୧ଶ୬୭

PRIORS OF LODERS UNDER THE ABBOT OF MONTEBOURG	
1109 to 1209 unknown	
Baldwin occurs	1209
Thomas	1287
Guillaume de Carenton	1312
Roger Hariel	1320
Robert Dore	1361
Sampson Trigal	1363
William Burnell,	1401 to 1414

VICARS OF LODERS	
John Sampson	date unknown
John Irlande,	1327
Henri de Whitford,	1353
Henri de Daunte,	
Hugh de Kymington,	
Richard Money,	
John Newman,	1383
Thomas Mere,	1384
Walter Cletheman,	1386
John Shaftesbury,	1400
Robert Gybbon,	1410
John Chulsagh,	1443
John Acculshawe,	
John Dremow,	1467
John Kepe,	1472
John Lane,	1494
John Walbef,	

Richard Whittock	1506
Richard Parker,	1533
Sylvester White,	1559
Richard Justice,	1579
William Odel,	1596
George Reeves-Legg	1611
Thomas Darby,	1670
William Dean,	1674
John Sutton,	1692
Robert Brown,	1733
Nathaniel Templeman,	1754
John Jones,	1783
Houlton Hartwell,	1813
Samuel Wallis,	1820
Francis Macarthy,	1835
Francis Dollman,	1848
William Curphey,	1859
Alfred Edersheim,	1876
John Stewart,	1883
J. Maclean,	1886
David Thomas,	1887
Arthur Bertram Hutton,	1914
Charles L.H. Beardmore,	1935
Charles Palmer,	1939
Oliver Leonard Willmott,	1947
Alexander L. Martin,	1984
Gregory Page-Turner,	1989

Historical background (1945–1953)

THE ROYAL FAMILY

November	1947	Princess Elizabeth marries Philip Mountbatten
December	1948	Prince Charles 'of Edinburgh' is born (p.82; p.185)
February	1950	King George VI sends a letter of congratulations on their diamond wedding to Eliza and William Marsh of Dottery (p.30)
February	1952	George VI – 1895–1952 – dies: Defender of the Faith, recognized by a British West Indian's eulogy (p.37)
	1953	Queen Mary of Teck, queen-consort of Great Britain – wife of George V – dies less than three months before the coronation of her grand-daughter Elizabeth (p.42)

BRITISH POLITICS

July	1945	Labour Government formed under Clement Attlee; he introduced the Austerity Programme with bread rationing introduced in 1946 and sweets still being rationed until 1953; Hugh Dalton was his first Chancellor of the Exchequer, followed by Stafford Cripps (p.154) and Hugh Gaitskell; the trade unions took the unprecedented step of imposing a voluntary wage freeze (see 'The unions and the C of E' p.31); Ernest Bevin as foreign secretary supported NATO and the development of nuclear weapons (with Edward Laskey, p.155)
November	1946	National Health Act
	1947	Nationalisation of the coal industry: one of Britain's worst winters
November	1948	Nationalisation of the Railways and Electricity (pps. 25–6; 28)
	1949	The UK Government devalues the £ by 30% Clothes Rationing ends
February	1950	Labour win the election, continuing under Clement Attlee (p.27)
October	1951	Conservative Government formed under Winston Churchill with R.A. Butler as Chancellor of the Exchequer (p.38)

NATIONAL and INTERNATIONAL EVENTS

1945   Germany surrenders, May 7th
       Atomic bombs dropped on Hiroshima and Nagasaki, 6th and 9th
       August
       Japan surrenders
1947   The British Empire ends in India: Nehru becomes Prime Minister
1948   *H.M.S. Vanguard* visits Weymouth: royal progress to Australia (p.22)
       Gandhi assassinated
       Formation of Israel, 14th May
       The population of Britain at its highest ever – the number of clergy
       lowest ever: 208 ordained in 1947 as against 590 in 1938 (p.51) Colonial
       food parcels arrive in Loders (pps. 23; 38–9) The Bridport Food Office
       set up: sausage queues and form-filling (pps. 23–4; 98; 106; 180).
       Nationalisation of the Railways and of Electricity (pps. 25–6; 28))
       The Olympic Games held in London
       In 1948–9 Britain spent £1,510 millions on tobacco, drink, cinemas,
       theatres and betting: the nation spent more in a year on matches
       than religion (p.28)
       1,500 ex-servicemen accepted for the Ministry at a cost of £1,000
       per head (p.51)
1949   Albert Einstein – 1879–1955 – German–Swiss–American–Jewish
       mathematical physicist: theory of relativity announced
       Scarlet Fever: (p.30)
       The Haigh Case – John Haigh, company director murders a widow
       and disposes of her body in sulphuric acid, leaving a recognizable
       plastic denture (p.33).
       George Orwell writes *1984*
1950   USSR claims atoms bomb 'success'
       Start of Korean War
1951   Festival of Britain on the South Bank of the Thames to mark the
       centenary of the Great Exhibition 1851, leaving the Festival Hall as a
       permanent legacy (p.34)
       South Africa disenfranchises 'coloured voters'
       First Eurovision Relay, aided by Richard Dimbleby – 1913–65
       – (p.35) 67 out of the 100 children are baptized, and 70 out of 100
       couples married in the Church of England; 70% of the population is
       nominally C of E (p.31)
1952   112 killed in Harrow train disaster – public concern about the state of
       the railway system (pps.26; 28)
       Nkrumah of Ghana (1909–1972) elected to parliament while still in jail;
       (1957 premier of first independent Commonwealth State). Eva Peron
       dies in Argentina, having campaigned successfully for women's
       suffrage.
       Mau Mau emergency in Kenya, led by Jomo Kenyatta advocating extreme
       nationalism Britain tests its first atomic bomb (see p.67 – 'Target for
       1951; p.165 – 'The war machine')
       Eisenhower wins US Presidential Election
       The Lynmouth Relief Fund set up (p.40)

Samuel Beckett writes *Waiting for Godot*
1953 Stalin dies
Salk vaccine successful in tests against polio
Housing Act passed by the Conservative Government to redeem election pledge of 300,000 houses per year, after failure of Attlee's government to reach its targets; by 1957 nearly 1.5 million houses and flats had been constructed (pps. 32; 34)
Everest conquered by Hillary and Tenzing, 29th May
Armistice in Korea
June: Coronation of Queen Elizabeth 2nd (pps. 44; 93; 149; 173; 198)

PEOPLE

Ernest Bevin 1881–1951 – foreign secretary in the Labour government 1945–1951 (p.155)

Miss Bryan – i/c Winston Churchill's underground signals HQ in Whitehall (p.196)

Julius Caesar – 100 or 102 – 44 BC – kept a diary: Jesus Christ didn't (p.62)

Sir Stafford Cripps – 1889–1952 – Labour statesman, Chancellor of the Exchequer, and economist (p.155)

Sir Roger De Coverley – from The Spectator 1711–1714 – would have approved of a Loders Christmas (p.6)

Demosthenes – 384-322 BC – an Athenian orator who declaimed to the sea as well as to the Senate (p.59)

Richard Dimbleby – 1913–1965 – BBC report in Berlin and Belsen; first live broadcast from the Soviet Union in 1961 (p.35)

Sir Francis Drake – c. 1540–1596 – died on an expedition to the West Indies, (having generally vexed the Spanish: prayer on entering Cadiz 1587 (p123.)

Bruno Enerts – Latvian – comes to Loders with daughter Aia (p.33)

Robert Gordon – jockey (p.96)

Thomas Hogarth – 1697–1764 – portrait-painter and cartoonist (p.73)

Mr Jeffries – lecturer at Bristol university (p.5)

Dr Samuel Johnson – 1709–1784 – his affection for pubs (p.172)

Sir Alan Herbert – 1890–1971 – *Punch* Cartoonist (p.22)

Detective Heslin CID – and the Haigh case (p.33)

Doctor Maxwell Jones – preaches for St. Lukestide (p.67)

Colonel Sir Edward Le Breton – Lord of the Manor of Loders (p.150); member of the Corps of Gentlemen-at-Arms for the funeral of Queen Victoria, and kings George V and VI (p.167); Commander of forces on HMS Nestor 1918 (p.173); awarded MVO in the Coronation Honours 1953 (p.29)

Sir Robert Gordon Menzies – Australian Prime Minister 1939–41; Leader of the Opposition 1943–1949 (p.32)

Sir Eustace Missenden – Chairman of the Railway Executive (p.25)

Mr Ernest Morris – champion bell-ringer (p.93)

Dame Isabel Nepean – built an elementary school for Loders in 1869 (p.174)

Sir Gordon Richards – 1904–1986 – Jockey: champion jockey 26 time and
    rode 4,870 winners; rode his first Derby winner in 1953 on Pinza, after
    which he was knighted (p.96)
Major General Sir Harry Smith – distinguished soldier of the Great War
    (p.24–5)
Mr. Tilley – King's Chorister of St George's Chapel, Windsor (p.100)
Richad Travers left £10 for a sermon in 1815 (p.9)
Captain Welstead – Boer War veteran and Frank Clark (p.25)

ENTERTAINMENT
Workers' Playtime (p.26)
Radiogram Recitals (p.5)
Radios were still 'wireless sets' (p.20)
Television superseded the cinema in the early 1950s: Coronation TV 3 in
    Uploders, 1 in Loders (p.42)
Wallace Productions Limited and *The Daily Mail* (p.5)
Talking films – Richard Dimbleby and Mrs Harry Legg (p.35)
Mr Dixon at the Weymouth Ritz (p.34)
Dick Barton – in Radio detective thrillers (p.184)
Musicians' Union – (p.35)
'Down Your Way' – Ralph Wightman the BBC godfather (p.28)
BBC Choir – (p.99)
Madame Tussaud's – (p.99)

THE CLERGY
The Archbishop of Canterbury – Geoffrey Fisher to Australia (p.32)
The Archbishop of York – 1942–55 Cyril Foster Garbett (p.31)
The Bishop of Salisbury: Geoffrey Charles Lester Lunt MC:
    Bishop from 1946–1948; died January (p.162)
    Dr William Louis Anderson DSO
    Bishop from 1949–1962 (pps. 25 & 161)
The Bishop of Sherborne: John Maurice Key (p.57 & p.161)
Bishop Ken – 1631–1711 – wrote 'Glory to Thee, my God, this night' and
    'Awake, my soul, and with the sun'; as Bishop of Winchester he refused to
    give up his house to Nell Gwynne when Charles 2nd visited (p.45)
The Bishop of Leicester – Dr Vernon Smith (p.162)
The Dean of Edinburgh – Very Rev Weston Henry Stewart (p.156)
Rev Reginald Allen, British Chaplain in Smyrna (p.158)
Bishop Lancelot Andrewes – 1555–1626 took part in the translation of the
    Authorized Version of the Bible published 1611 – 'one of the most
    learned theologians of his time'; finally Bishop of Winchester in 1618
    (p. 3)
Rev Lancelot Andrewes – of Oriel College, Oxford (p.3)
Admiral Andrewes – ADC to King George VI (p.3)
Rev Beardmore – Vicar of Loders 1935–1939 (p.170)
Canon Buckley – Precentor of Chester Cathedral, then Vicar of Gulval in
    Cornwall (p.104)
Rev B.N. Carver – Vicar of Bradpole (p.170)

Canon Clare – Chaplain of the Bridport Hospitals and Rector of Bridport (p.168)

Rev Cox – Rector of Askerswell in 1842 – with Livingstone to Africa (p.40)

Canon Daniell – Rector of Askerswell. Resigned January 1952 (p.16); bees; funeral (p. 142–4)

Dr. Edersheim – Vicar of Loders 1876–1883 – wrote erudite theological books about the Jews, and a forerunner of the *Parish Notes;* had Dottery church built(p.6)

Rev Hutton – Vicar of Loders 1914–1935 (p.170)

Rev Page-Turner – Vicar of Loders 1989- (p.151)

Rev Palmer – Vicar of Loders 1939–1947 (p.156)

Dr Selwyn – Dean of Winchester (p.171)